Creando Abundancia con EFT
Técnica de Liberación Emocional

Tapeos prácticos para aplicar la Técnica de Liberación Emocional para crear mas abundancia y prosperidad..

Por Carla Valencia

http://www.autoayuda-eft.com

Copyright © 2008 by Carla Valencia. Todos los derechos mundiales reservados. Ninguna parte de este libro electrónico puede ser copiada y/o comercializada. Reproducida, almacenada o transmitida por ningún medio electrónico, mecánico, fotocopiadora, grabadora o de otra manera, sin la autorización por escrito del autor.

AUG 2 5 2012

Renuncia Legal de Responsabilidad

La información contenida en el presente ejemplar está desarrollada solamente con fines educativos. Este libro no es un sustituto para aconsejar, la evaluación psicológica o la psicoterapia. Este libro electrónico esta diseñado para proporcionar la información en vista del tema cubierto. Se vende con la comprensión que el autor no está rindiendo servicios psicológicos. Si se requieren los servicios psicológicos, por favor entre en contacto con su profesional de salud mental para tales servicios.

Agradecimientos

Quiero agradecer especialmente a mi marido por el apoyo que me brindó para que este libro electrónico sea posible y por el diseño de gráficos y edición de videos.

Contenido

INTRODUCCIÓN 8

CAPITULO 1: "QUE ES LA TÉCNICA DE LIBERACIÓN EMOCIONAL" 12

CAPÍTULO 2: "EL PROTOCOLO ABREVIADO DE LAS TÉCNICAS DE LIBERACIÓN EMOCIONAL" ... 15

    PUNTOS DEL TRATAMIENTO DE EFT 15
    COMO TAPEAR LOS PUNTOS PARA EL TRATAMIENTO DE EFT 16

CAPITULO 3: "RELACIÓN CON EL DINERO" 20

CAPITULO 4: "COMO UTILIZAR EFT PARA CREAR MAS ABUNDANCIA DE DINERO EN NUESTRA VIDA" 24

    LIBERAR LOS MIEDOS 27
    1) Liberar la necesiad de mantener mi presente identidad finaciera *28*
    2) Resistencia al cambio *30*
    3) Miedo de lo que los demás pensarán de mi si cambio *32*
    4) Miedo a lo Nuevo y desconocido *34*
    5) Miedo de ganar mas que suficiente dinero *36*
    EL PODER 38
    1) El poder corrompe a las personas y los vuelve déspotas *40*
    LOS QUE TIENEN MUCHO DINERO ES PORQUE ROBARON Y HACEN TRAMPA 42

1) Las personas que tienen mucho dinero es porque robaron y hacen trampa 44
EL DINERO ES SUCIO Y ES LA CAUSA DE TODO LO MALO 46
1) El dinero es sucio y la causa de todo lo malo 47
ES MEJOR DAR QUE RECIBIR 49
1) Es mejor dar que recibir 51
CAPÍTULO 5 : "MAS CREENCIAS QUE NOS BLOQUEAN" 53

Creencia: El dinero no es importante 55
1) El dinero no es importante 57
2) Para ser bueno debo ser pobre 61
3) Si tengo mas dinero que otros, ellos no tendrán suficiente 63
4) Para tener mucho dinero debo trabajar duro y sacrificar muchas cosas 65
5) Debo ser humilde y no esperar ninguna recompensa por mis esfuerzos 67
6) Los que tienen mucho dinero lo hicieron a expensas de los demás 69
7) Hay que ahorrar dinero por si algo malo sucede 71
8) Esta bien gastar dinero para mi familia pero si lo hago para mi soy egoista 73
9) Secuencia de tapeo para la creencia: No merezco tener mucho dinero 75
10) El dinero escasea 77
11) Hay que nacer con dinero para ser rico 79

12) Mi familia y amigos me van a rechazar si tengo mucho dinero 81
13) Las personas espirituales no les importa el dinero 83
14) Se necesita dinero para hacer mas dinero 85
15) Nunca tengo suficiente dinero 87
16) Nunca puedo tener lo que quiero 89
17) No merezco ser feliz y exitoso 91
18) Necesito que alguien me salve de mi situacion financiera 93
19) Secuencia de tapeo para la creencia: Si tengo mucho dinero traicionaré a mi padre que nunca lo tuvo 95
20) Tener mucho dinero complica la vida 97

CONCLUSIÓN **99**

BIBLIOGRAFIA: **100**

OTROS LIBROS POR CARLA VALENCIA 101
ACERCA DE CARLA VALENCIA 102

Introducción

"La abundancia no es algo que usted adquiere. Es algo con lo que nos conectamos". Wayne Dyer.

Esta usted conectado o desconectado a la abundancia?. Tiene una mentalidad de escasez o de abundancia?. Muchos de nosotros creemos que la abundancia cuando nos referimos preferentemente al dinero es un tema de suerte. Nos lamentamos de no haber nacido en una familia adinerada o que no nos ganamos el loto y muchas cosas más.

La abundancia de dinero no es cuestión de suerte. La abundancia de es una conexión que tenemos con el mismo.
Que piensa usted acerca del dinero?. Que piensa acerca de la gente con mucho dinero? ¿Cuál es el concepto que usted tiene del poder?.

Debido a que la abundancia de dinero no es suerte sería interesante comenzar a hacernos ciertas preguntas al respecto. Para poder conectarnos con el dinero y la abundancia en general necesitamos estar claros con respecto a las ideas que tenemos del mismo.

Antes de comenzar con estos cuestionamientos me gustaría dar una explicación sobre que es la Técnica de Liberación Emocional para todos aquellos que no tienen experiencia utilizando la misma.

Para las personas nuevas en este tema aconsejo que bajen el manual gratis de EFT. También pueden obtener mi libro de Técnicas de Liberación Emocional: EFT Sanación Emocional, donde explico que es EFT, como se utiliza y variadas aplicaciones de las mismas en: http://www.autoayuda-eft.com/libro-de-tecnicas-de-liberacion-emocional-espanol.htm.

He dividido este libro electrónico en dos partes principales.

1. En la primera parte explicaré que es la Técnica de Liberación Emocional en forma abreviada porqué vamos a utilizarla con el tema de la abundancia de dinero.

2. En la Segunda parte le daré al lector una serie de preguntas para que pueda comenzar a tener claro cual es su relación con el dinero y una vez finalizado esto le daré tapeos para que pueda comenzar a utilizar la Técnica de Liberación Emocional para poder lograr mas abundancia de dinero en su vida.

Sugerencia para utilizar este libro: Creo que la mejor manera de utilizar este libro electrónico para tener resultados exitosos es seguir los siguientes pasos:

1. Asegúrese que sabe como utilizar la Técnica de Liberación Emocional
2. Conteste las preguntas sobre la relación con el dinero.

3. Tome una secuencia de tapeo, por ejemplo: "Secuencia de tapeo liberar la necesidad de mantener mi presente identidad financiera". Tapee esta secuencia hasta que la intensidad llegue a cero. Anote los pensamientos e imagines que le surgen mientras tapea. Antes de pasar a la otra secuencia de tapeo asegúrese de haber tapeado las imagines y pensamientos que surgieron.

4. Luego pase a la siguiente secuencia de tapeo y así sucesivamente.

¿Cómo notará los cambios en su vida? De muchas manera. Algunas veces estos cambios son muy sutiles por eso es importante la auto observación. Notará que se siente más tranquilo y relajado. Que sus ingresos aumentan de formas inesperadas. Que no se siente tan preocupado por las cuentas que tiene que pagar. Que se asocia con personas con dinero y no se siente incómodo y muchos cambios mas.

Visite mi video de como crear mas abundancia con EFT: http://www.autoayuda-eft.com/video-eft-abundancia.htm. El mismo le ayudará a despejar algunos conflictos.

Recuerde que lo mejor es perseverar y llegar a la raíz del problema. Todos los tapeos en este libro electrónico fueron creados y practicados por mi con notables resultados. Si mientras está utilizando las secuencias de tapeo tiene problemas y no puede avanzar o preguntas y dudas no dude en contactarme: webmaster@autoayuda-eft.com . Si nota cambios y le gustaría compartirlos con mucho gusto los publicaré en mi página, desde ya su nombre será mantenido en anonimato si así lo desea.

Deseándole abundancia y prosperidad en su vida,

Carla Valencia. http://www-autoayuda-eft.com

Capitulo 1: "Que es la Técnica de Liberación Emocional"

Gary Craig desarrolló la Técnica de Liberación Emocional durante 1990. Esta técnica es utilizada cuando queremos equilibrar emociones negativas y simplifica TFT (Terapia del Campo del Pensamiento) creada por Rogers Callahan. Tiene sus raíces en la Medicina China y la ciencia moderna de Kinesiología.

La técnica de liberación emocional dice que toda emoción negativa se desarrolla cuando un individuo atraviesa experiencias negativas. Por lo tanto la persona va a sentir emociones negativas respondiendo a dicha experiencia y esto va a crear una programación inapropiada dentro de su cuerpo.

El sistema energético va a desarmonizarse debido a estas emociones negativas y para poder remover estas respuestas negativas es necesario sanar las emociones involucradas. La diferencia principal entre EFT y TFT es su aplicación.

Estimulando ciertos puntos energéticos se le pide a la persona que se conecte con el dolor físico o emocional y se comienza el tapeo. Esto permite que la persona libere las emociones negativas o el dolor que está padeciendo. En otras palabras, este tapeo produce una harmonización de la energía en el cuerpo.

La Técnica de Liberación Emocional establece que...

- "La causa de todas las emociones negativas es una desarmonización del sistema energético del cuerpo."

Debido a que las enfermedades y los dolores físicos obviamente están conectados con nuestras emociones, la siguiente afirmación es probada como verdadera:

- "Nuestras emociones negativas no resueltas son el mayor contribuyente de la mayoría de nuestras enfermedades y dolores."

La Técnica de Liberación Emocional puede ser aplicada en cualquier lugar. Cuando siente una emoción negativa o positiva ésta se refleja dentro de su cuerpo. Ha sido aplicada exitosamente para resolver problemas emocionales y de salud mental incluyendo:

- Ansiedad y estrés.
- Miedos y fobias.
- Depresión.
- Baja autoestima.
- Problemas de relaciones.
- Abusos y traumas.

Ha sido probada como muy efectiva en problemas físicos incluyendo:

- Problemas respiratorios.

- Problemas de peso.
- Alergias.
- Asma.
- Insomnio.
- Dolores de cabeza.
- Enfermedades crónicas y mucho más.

Es también muy efectiva para la abundancia, los deportes, el trabajo y la vida personal.

Cualquiera puede utilizar la Técnica de Liberación Emocional, usted no necesita especializarse yendo a una Universidad. Simplemente necesita sentido común y decisión.

Sin embargo es aconsejable consultar a un experto en el tema si su problema es muy fuerte o complicado para resolver. Este sería el caso de traumas o abusos que son muy dolorosos de enfrentar sin ayuda profesional.

Capítulo 2: "El protocolo abreviado de las Técnicas de Liberación Emocional"

A continuación voy a describir cual es el protocolo abreviado para poder utilizar la Técnica de Liberación Emocional:

Puntos del tratamiento de EFT

En la Técnica de Liberación Emocional estos puntos son estimulados cuando se tapean. Recuerde que tapear significa dar golpecitos con los dedos para estimular los meridianos. La fuerza del tapeo no debe ser extremadamente fuerte, sino de una manera que se sienta confortable.

Por favor diríjase a la pagina donde presento las fotos para mas claridad: http://www.autoayuda-eft.com/que-es-eft.htm

12 = Punto de Karate (PK) - es el parte de la mano que se utiliza en la práctica del Karate.

0 = Punto del pecho (clavícula)- En el ángulo formado por la clavícula y el esternón. Suavemente ponga los dedos y sienta la parte mas blanda.

1 = Ceja (CJ) – Donde comienza su ceja.

2 = Lado del ojo (LO) – Sobre el hueso que está al lado del ojo.

3 = Debajo del ojo (DO) – Justo debajo del ojo.

4 = Debajo de la nariz (BN) – Entre la nariz y el labio superior

5 = Debajo de la boca (mentón) – entre el mentón y el labio inferior

7 = Debajo del brazo – siguiendo la línea de los pezones en el lado del cuerpo

Como tapear los puntos para el tratamiento de EFT

Consulte por favor los siguientes videos si necesita ayuda en como aplicar la técnica de liberación emocional para verlo en forma práctica:

Video # 1: http://www.autoayuda-eft.com/eft-pasos.htm

Video # 2: http://www.autoayuda-eft.com/eft-pasos-abreviados.htm

Una manera corta de realizar el protocolo sería de la siguiente manera:

1. Crear la frase
2. Medir la intensidad: De 0 a 10
3. Crear la frase que tapeara en cada punto

Comenzamos entonces a tapear el punto de karate repitiendo tres veces:

> *"Aunque (inserte aquí el problema), yo, profundamente me acepto a mi misma."*

Luego hacemos la secuencia:

1 = Lado de la ceja.
2 = Lado del ojo.
3 = Debajo del ojo.
4 = Debajo de la nariz
5 = Debajo de la boca
6 = Clavícula –
7 = Debajo del brazo
8 = sobre la cabeza

Note que la manera abreviada es ignorar el procedimiento 9 gama. Testeamos la intensidad del problema, si no ha bajado a cero hacemos la secuencia con la frase: "todavía"

> *"Aunque todavía (inserte el problema), yo, profundamente me acepto a mi misma."*

Luego hacemos la secuencia con la palabra "restante":

1 = Lado de la ceja. (inserte el problema) restante
2 = Lado del ojo. (inserte el problema) restante
3 = Debajo del ojo. (inserte el problema) restante
4 = Debajo de la nariz (inserte el problema) restante
5 = Debajo de la boca (inserte el problema) restante
6 = Clavícula – (inserte el problema) restante
7 = Debajo del brazo (inserte el problema) restante
8 = sobre la cabeza (inserte el problema) restante

Esta sería una manera de utilizar EFT en forma abreviada sin el procedimiento 9 gama. De acuerdo a mi experiencia yo utilizo esta secuencia abreviada para eliminar emociones diarias sobre problemas que surgen en el día.

Sin embargo, si necesito trabajar sobre un problema más dificultoso, utilizo la secuencia completa incluyendo el procedimiento gama. En el caso de que usted se encuentre en un lugar donde no pueda repetir las frases en voz alta, simplemente imagine los puntos y tapee con sus pensamientos realizando el procedimiento abreviado.

Debido a que la palabra dinero tiene mucha connotación emocional, aplicar las Técnicas de Liberación Emocional es uno de los recursos más exitosos. La relación que tenemos con el dinero está determinada básicamente por creencias y emociones.

Las creencias las hemos obtenido de nuestros familiares, amigos, la sociedad y la vida en general. Las emociones surgirán a consecuencia de estas creencias y si estas creencias son negativas nuestras emociones también lo serán.

Para aclararlo un poco más:

Supongamos que nuestra madre siempre nos dijo que las personas con mucho dinero son déspotas y arrogantes. De tanto escuchar esto y experimentarlo constantemente por eventos que le sucedían a nuestra madre, tomamos estas creencias como propias.

Debido a que esta creencia es negativa y está asociada a nuestra madre nos produce una emoción negativa porque sentimos que "estas personas con mucho dinero eran déspotas y arrogantes con nuestra madre".

Luego cuando nos volvemos adultos seguimos manteniendo estas creencias que nos van a llevar a crear una realidad que no queremos. Las consecuencias serán:

- No quiero tener mucho dinero porque los que lo tienen son déspotas y arrogantes
- No quiero tener mucho dinero porque sino lastimare a mi madre

Cuando aplicamos la Técnica de Liberación emocional a estas creencias nos liberamos de la connotación negativa y despejamos nuestra mente para poder ver esta creencia de otra manera.

Es decir podemos darnos cuenta de repente que a pesar de esta creencia que tenía nuestra madre hemos conocido numerosas personas con mucho dinero que no son déspotas ni arrogantes.

Por eso creo que la Técnica de liberación emocional es una de las mas efectivas herramientas para liberarnos de conceptos erróneos y mitos que tenemos acerca del dinero que no nos dejan vivir con abundancia y felicidad.

Capitulo 3: "Relación con el dinero"

"El dinero es un resultado, la abundancia es un resultado, la salud es un resultado, la enfermedad es un resultado, su peso es un resultado. Vivimos en un mundo de causa y efecto". Harv Eker

La relación que tenemos con el dinero va a ser un determinante de como nos relacionamos con él y de la cantidad de dinero que nos vamos a permitir tener. Como en cualquier relación con una persona nuestras creencias y preconceptos determinarán el éxito o fracaso de esa relación.

Muchos de nosotros fuimos educados con la creencia que la abundancia de dinero es simplemente suerte o trabajo muy duro. Si seguimos pensando de esta manera nunca podremos tener abundancia de dinero puesto que consideramos que no tenemos suerte y si lo pensamos bien no queremos trabajar muy duro.

Sin embargo la vida demuestra lo contrario. Hay personas que parecen atraer el dinero muy fácilmente y otras que aunque no trabajan muy duro tienen mucho dinero.

Creo que existen muchos conflictos con la palabra dinero y estos conflictos surgen debido a como hemos sido educados, lo que nuestros padres y familiares e incluso amigos nos transmitieron.

Su situación financiera esta relacionada con sus

Pensamientos -> creencias -> emociones que producen su comportamiento.

Que piensa usted acerca del dinero?. Tal vez usted contestaría que quiere tener mucho dinero pero a la vez tiene miedo porque algo malo va a pasar. O tal vez diga que tener mucho dinero no es bueno pero a la vez necesita el dinero. Todos estos conflictos de pensamientos crean confusión y si estamos confundidos no vamos a poder crear el dinero que queremos.

Yo crecí en una familia donde mi padre era el proveedor y mi madre ama de casa. En casa creían fuertemente tanto mi madre como mi padre que la mujer no debe ganar dinero y si lo hace se quedará soltera y sola. Mi padre siempre me dijo: "No te preocupes por el dinero un hombre que te quiera te lo va a dar".

Antes mencionamos que los pensamientos, creencias y emociones producen un comportamiento.

- Mis pensamientos eran: "No debo ganar dinero".
- Mis creencias: "Si gano dinero me voy a quedar soltera y sola". "Un hombre que me quiera me va dar dinero".
- Mis emociones: "Miedo a ganar dinero".
- Mi comportamiento: "Buscaré situaciones que me lleven a no ganar dinero".

Todo esto por supuesto es muy inconsciente y lo veremos claramente cuando decidamos cuestionar nuestras creencias y pensamientos.

Por eso creo que es fundamental un poco de introspección y revisión de nuestras creencias, pensamientos y emociones para poder darnos cuenta cuales son los bloqueos que no nos permiten tener el dinero que deseamos.

A continuación voy a realizarle algunas preguntas que lo ayudaran a decidir:

Preguntas sobre el dinero en si mismo:

1. Cree usted que el dinero es sucio, alguna vez le dijeron en su casa que se lave las manos porque tocó dinero?
2. Cree usted que el dinero corrompe a las personas?
3. Cree usted que el dinero no es fácil de conseguir?
4. Cree usted que tiene que trabajar muy duro para tener mucho dinero?
5. Cree usted que la mujer no debe ganar mucho dinero?
6. Cree usted que el hombre debe ganar mucho dinero?
7. Como interpreta usted la frase bíblica: es mas fácil que un camello entre por el ojo de una aguja que un rico en el Reino de los Cielos?

8. Cree usted que los que no tienen dinero se irán al cielo?
9. Cree usted que tener mucho dinero destruye a la familia?
10. Preguntas con respecto a los ricos:
11. Cree usted que los ricos son ricos simplemente porque heredaron el dinero?
12. Cree usted que los ricos son insensibles y avaros?
13. Cree usted que los ricos explotan a los pobres?
14. Cree usted que los ricos son infelices, divorciados y viciosos?
15. Se siente usted inferior a los ricos?
16. Cree usted que nunca podrá ser rico?

Si usted a contestado que si a más de dos o tres de estas preguntas indudablemente tiene creencias negativas que no le están permitiendo abrirse a recibir abundancia de dinero.

Capitulo 4: "Como utilizar EFT para crear mas abundancia de dinero en nuestra vida"

"Cuando la mente subconciente tiene que elegir entre lógica y emociones, siempre elige las emociones."
Harv Eker.

La mejor manera de utilizar la Técnica de Liberación Emocional para crear más abundancia de dinero es aclarar todos nuestros conflictos. Uno de los conflictos más inconcientes que tenemos que nos impiden avanzar con este tema es nuestra identidad. Estamos totalmente identificados con el tipo de persona que somos.

Por ejemplo: si usted nunca tuvo mucho dinero se identificará con esto y le parecerá muy raro y a veces imposible imaginarse a si mismo con mucho dinero o con más que suficiente dinero.

Cuando transitamos este camino surgen miedo relacionados a nuestra identidad. No queremos perderla, todos nos conocen con esta identidad. Si la perdemos cambiándola aunque sea para bien tal vez perderemos el amor de los demás. Nuestors amigos y familiars comenzarán a decir: "El o ella no era así, mira como cambio! Que le pasó? Etc. Etc.

Por eso el querer abrise a la prosperidad es una decisión. Al tomar esta decisión debemos estar seguros de que aunque perderemos nuestra identidad anterior vamos a crear una nueva que nos llevará a algo mejor.

Por lo tanto sería muy importante que nos volvamos concientes de cómo nos saboteamos. Los aspectos más importantes a tomar en cuenta serán:

1. Estar dispuestos a cambiar nuestra identidad (autoimagen),
2. Reconocer nuestra manera en que nos saboteamos y
3. Observar nuestra resistencia al cambio.

Si está lleyendo esta página creo que ya habrá contestado las preguntas que realicé en el capitulo anterior. Contestar estas preguntas no lo llevará a crear más dinero. Profundizar las mismas y eliminar las negatividades lo llevarán a tener mas paz con respecto a la palabra dinero y por lo tanto le sera mas fácil abrirse a recibir abundancia.

Usted podrá aplicar EFT a estas negatividades y bloqueos y de esta manera su percepción con respecto al dinero irá cambiando y podrá crear una relación más positiva con el mismo.

El cambio no se realizará de la noche a la mañana, pero gradualmente comenzará a notar que ya no siente tanta presión con respecto al dinero y que cada día se permite recibir más sin culpas y miedos.

Cada uno a nacido en lugares diferentes y tenido experiencias diferentes con respecto al dinero por eso es que no existe una fórmula mágica que resuelva todos los conflictos.

Me gustaría enfocarme en algunos conceptos que son similares en todos lados, que formarían parte por asi decirlo del inconciente colectivo. Una vez que usted pueda resolver estos conflictos o ideas podrá comenzar a enfocarse en temas muy personales y únicos acerca de su vida.

A continuación voy especificar estos conceptos.

Liberar los miedos

"La emoción mas vieja y fuerte de la humnaidad es el miedo."
H.P. Lovecraft

Todo cambio nos produce miedos. Sentimos miedo a lo desconocido y nos sentimos incómodos. Los principales miedos que surgen cuando comenzamos a cambiar actitudes con respecto al dinero son:

- Miedo de cambiar nuestra identidad financiera
- Miedo al cambio en general
- Miedo a lo que los demás van a pensar de usted
- Resistencia y apego a lo viejo por miedo a lo nuevo y desconocido

Las técnicas de liberación emocional son una excelente herramienta para liberar estos tipos de miedos. Vamos a ver a continuación como las podemos aplicar. Lo mejor es comenzar liberando la necesidad de nuestro apego a nuestra identidad finaciera y de sentir resistencia al cambio.

1) Liberar la necesiad de mantener mi presente identidad finaciera

Repita la siguiente frase tres veces mientras tapea en el punto de karate:

"Aunque yo siento miedo de liberar mi necesidad de mantener mi presente identidad financiera yo profundamente y completamente me amo y me acepto a mi misma"

1 = Lado de la ceja – "este miedo de liberar esta necesidad"

2 = Lado del ojo – "este miedo de liberar esta necesidad"

3 = Debajo del ojo – "este miedo de liberar esta necesidad"

4 = Debajo de la nariz – "este miedo de liberar esta necesidad"

5 = Debajo de la boca – "este miedo de liberar esta necesidad"

6 = Clavícula – "este miedo de liberar esta necesidad"

7 = Debajo del brazo – "este miedo de liberar esta necesidad"

8= Sobre la cabeza – "este miedo de liberar esta necesidad"

Medimos nuestra intensidad, simplemente pensamos en que vamos a tener una nueva identidad financiera y medimos el miedo. Seguimos tapeando hasta que baje a cero.

Recuerde que si necesita seguir tapeando debe agregar la frase: "Aunque todavia siento miedo de liberar mi necesidad de mantener mi presente identidad financiera yo profundamente me acepto a mi misma" y luego en los puntos del cuerpo: "restante miedo de liberar esta necesidad". Si no recuerda como hacerlo mire el video 2: http://www.autoayuda-eft.com/EFT-pasos-abreviados.htm.

Recuerde que cada vez que realiza un tapeo van a surgir imágenes o pensamientos nuevos con respecto al tema . Debemos tapear todo lo nuevo que surja. Escriba a continuación todos los pensamientos e imágnes que surjan mientras tapea:

1 -

2 -

3 -

4 -

5 -

6 -

7 -

8 -

9 -

10 –

2) Resistencia al cambio

Repita la siguiente frase tres veces mientras tapea en el punto de karate:

"Aunque yo estoy resistiendo cambiar yo profundamente me acepto a mi misma"

1 = Lado de la ceja – "esta resistencia de cambiar"
2 = Lado del ojo – "esta necesidad de seguir igual"
3 = Debajo del ojo – "este miedo de cambiar"
4 = Debajo de la nariz – "esta resistencia de cambiar"
5 = Debajo de la boca – "esta necesidad de seguir igual"
6 = Clavícula – "este miedo de cambiar"
7 = Debajo del brazo – "esta resistencia de cambiar"
8 = Sobre la cabeza – "esta resistencia de cambiar"

Medimos nuestra intensidad, simplemente pensamos en que vamos a cambiar y medimos el miedo.
Seguimos tapeando hasta que baje a cero. Recuerde que cada vez que realiza un tapeo van a surgir imagines o pensamientos nuevos con respecto al tema .Debemos tapear todo lo nuevo que surja.

Escriba a continuación todos los pensamientos e imágnes que surjan mientras tapea:

1 -
2 -
3 -

4 -
5 -
6 -
7 -
8 -
9 -
10 -

3) Miedo de lo que los demás pensarán de mi si cambio

Repita la siguiente frase tres veces mientras tapea en el punto de karate:

"Aunque yo siento miedo de lo que los demás van a pensar de mi si cambio, yo profunda y completamente me acepto a mi misma"

1 = Lado de la ceja – "este miedo de lo que los demás van a pensar de mi"
2 = Lado del ojo – "este miedo de lo que los demás van a pensar de mi"
3 = Debajo del ojo – "este miedo de lo que los demás van a pensar de mi"
4 = Debajo de la nariz – "este miedo de lo que los demás van a pensar de mi"
5 = Debajo de la boca – "este miedo de lo que los demás van a pensar de mi"
6 = Clavícula – "este miedo de lo que los demás van a pensar de mi"
7 = Debajo del brazo – "este miedo de lo que los demás van a pensar de mi"
8 = Sobre la cabeza – "este miedo de lo que los demás van a pensar de mi"

Medimos nuestra intensidad, simplemente pensamos en que vamos a cambiar y medimos el miedo. Seguimos tapeando hasta que baje a cero. Recuerde que cada vez que realiza un tapeo van a surgir imagines o pensamientos nuevos con respecto al tema . Debemos tapear todo lo nuevo que surja.

Escriba a continuación todos los pensamientos e imágnes que surjan mientras tapea:

1 -

2 -

3 -

4 -

5 -

6 -

7 -

8 -

9 -

10 -

4) Miedo a lo Nuevo y desconocido

Repita la siguiente frase tres veces mientras tapea en el punto de karate:

"Aunque yo siento miedo a lo nuevo y desconocido, resisto el cambio financiero y vivo apegado a lo viejo, yo profundamente me acepto a mi misma"

1 = Lado de la ceja – "este miedo a lo nuevo y desconocido"

2 = Lado del ojo – "resisto el cambio financiero"

3 = Debajo del ojo – "este miedo a lo nuevo y desconocido"

4 = Debajo de la nariz – "resisto el cambio financiero"

5 = Debajo de la boca – "este miedo a lo nuevo y desconocido"

6 = Clavícula – "resisto el cambio financiero"

7 = Debajo del brazo – "este miedo a lo nuevo y desconocido"

8 = Sobre la cabeza – "resisto el cambio financiero"

Medimos nuestra intensidad. Seguimos tapeando hasta que baje a cero. Recuerde que cada vez que realiza un tapeo van a surgir imagines o pensamientos nuevos con respecto al tema .Debemos tapear todo lo nuevo que surja.

Escriba a continuación todos los pensamientos e imágnes que surjan mientras tapea:

1 -
2 -
3 -
4 -
5 -
6 -
7 -
8 -
9 -
10 –

5) Miedo de ganar mas que suficiente dinero

Repita la siguiente frase tres veces mientras tapea en el punto de karate:

"Aunque yo siento miedo de ganar mas que suficiente dinero, yo profundamente me acepto a mi misma"

1 = Lado de la ceja – "este miedo de ganar mas que suficiente dinero "
2 = Lado del ojo – "este miedo de ganar mas que suficiente dinero"
3 = Debajo del ojo – "este miedo de ganar mas que suficiente dinero "
4 = Debajo de la nariz – "este miedo de ganar mas que suficiente dinero"
5 = Debajo de la boca – "este miedo de ganar mas que suficiente dinero"
6 = Clavícula – "este miedo de ganar mas que suficiente dinero"
7 = Debajo del brazo – "este miedo de ganar mas que suficiente dinero"
8 = Sobre la cabeza – "este miedo de ganar mas que suficiente dinero"

Medimos nuestra intensidad, simplemente pensamos en que vamos a cambiar y medimos el miedo. Seguimos tapeando hasta que baje a cero. Recuerde que cada vez que realiza un tapeo van a surgir

imagines o pensamientos nuevos con respecto al tema
. Debemos tapear todo lo nuevo que surja.

Escriba a continuación todos los pensamientos e imágnes que surjan mientras tapea:

1 -

2 -

3 -

4 -

5 -

6 -

7 -

8 -

9 -

10 –

El poder

"Si el poder corrompe, el no tener poder lo transforma a usted en una persona pura?. Harry Shearer.

La palabra poder es una palabra muy mal interpretada mundialmente. Cada vez que escuchamos esta palabra nos ponemos tensos porque inmediatamente la relacionamos con los politicos y opresores.

Generalmente asociamos poder con opresores y déspotas y con mucho dinero. Por esa razón nos da mucho miedo tener mucho dinero porque no queremos ser poderosos. Como esta palabra esta ligada a la corrupción no queremos volvermos corruptos. Nuestro diálogo interno es : "Si tengo mucho dinero me voy a volver poderoso y voy a ser un corrupto y déspota. Por lo tanto prefiero no tenerlo."

Creo que existen muchas personas poderosas que no son corruptas ni déspotas por ejemplo el Daila Lama. Entonces nos damos cuenta que el poder no es malo , una persona puede tener mucho poder y ser muy generosa y amorosa y otra persona puede tener mucho poder y ser corrupta y déspota. Cuando logremos cambiar esta percepción distorcionada podremos sentirnos más seguros de que el poder no nos va a corropmer ni va a volvernos déspotas.

El dinero está muy asociado a la palabra "poder" por lo tanto el primer paso para poder cambiar esta percepción errónea es enfocarnos en nuestras creencias con respecto al poder y los poderosos.

Una vez que logramos liberarnos de la cognotación negativa sobre el poder vamos a perder el miedo de que si tenemos mucho dinero vamos a ser poderosos. El ser poderosos no nos va a molestar puesto que sabremos que somos buenas personas y que vamos a poder manejar nuestro poder de una manera apropiada.

1) El poder corrompe a las personas y los vuelve déspotas

Repita la siguiente frase tres veces mientras tapea en el punto de karate:

"Aunque yo creo que el poder corrompe a las personas y las vuelve déspotas, yo profunda y completamente me amo y me acepto a mi misma"

1 = Lado de la ceja – "esta creencia, el poder corrompe a las personas y las vuelve déspotas"

2 = Lado del ojo – "esta creencia, el poder corrompe a las personas y las vuelve déspotas"

3 = Debajo del ojo – "esta creencia, el poder corrompe a las personas y las vuelve déspotas"

4 = Debajo de la nariz – "esta creencia, el poder corrompe a las personas y las vuelve despotas"

5 = Debajo de la boca – "esta creencia, el poder corrompe a las personas y las vuelve déspotas"

6 = Clavícula – "esta creencia, el poder corrompe a las personas y las vuelve despotas"

7 = Debajo del brazo – "esta creencia, el poder corrompe a las personas y las vuelve déspotas"

8= Sobre la cabeza – "esta creencia el poder corrompe a las personas y las vuelve déspotas"

Respiramos profundamente. Cuando terminamos, medimos la intensidad. ¿Sigue usted pensando que " el poder corrompe a las personas y las vuelve déspotas "? Repita en voz alta: "el poder corrompe a las personas y las vuelve déspotas". Si la intensidad no ha bajado a cero continuamos tapeando. Y así sucesivamente seguimos midiendo la intensidad hasta que llegue a cero.

Mientras tapeamos esta creencia seguramente surgiran otras creencias o imagines o recuerdos con respecto al poder. Debe por lo tanto tapear con todo esto .

Escriba a continuación todos los pensamientos e imágnes que surjan mientras tapea:

1 -

2 -

3 -

4 -

5 -

6 -

7 -

8 -

9 -

10 –

Los que tienen mucho dinero es porque robaron y hacen trampa

Cuál es nuestra actitud frente a las personas que tienen mucho dinero?. No le ha sucedido a usted ver a alguien en un auto caro y pensar: "Qué se cree que es el dueño de la calle? Seguro que robó o hizo trampa para poder comprar su auto".

Creo que a veces los medios de comunicación influencian mucho los pensamientos que tenemos con respecto a los ricos . En general en las películas el protagonista malo es el que tiene mucho dinero y el bueno es el que no lo tiene.

Cuando nos compremetamos en una película o serie casi siempre estamos esperando que el progagonista con mucho dinero caiga. Ha pensado alguna vez en cómo esto afecta sus creencias con respecto al dinero? Todos queremos ser buenas personas y si tenemos el concepto de que los ricos son malos, tramposos y seguramente robaron para lograr el dinero que tienen por supuesto que no vamos a querer ser como ellos. Por lo tanto no vamos a querer tener el dinero.

Sería también interesante pensar sobre parientes o amigos o incluso conocidos que tienen mucho dinero. Como reaccionamos ante eso. Muchos comentarios con respecto a esto son:

- "Tiene mucho dinero pero no es feliz".

- "Mirá como destruyó a su familia por culpa del dinero".
- "Es un egoista y tacaño".
- "Cree que me va a poder comprar con el dinero", etc.

Todos somos concientes de que en le mundo existen personas que robaron e hicieron trampa para tener mucho dinero. Pero también existen personas que no robaron ,ni hicieron trampa y tienen mucho dinero.

Es necesario entonces que comencemos a cambiar estas percepciones con respecto a las personas que tienen mucho dinero.

Una vez que logramos liberarnos de la cognotación negativa de que para poder tener dinero hay que robar y hacer trampa va a ser mas fácil para nostros permitirnos recibir más dinero puesto que sabremos que esto no es verdad.

1) Las personas que tienen mucho dinero es porque robaron y hacen trampa

Repita la siguiente frase tres veces mientras tapea en el punto de karate:

"Aunque yo creo que las personas que tienen mucho dinero es porque robaron y hacen trampa , yo profundamente me acepto a mi misma"

1 = Lado de la ceja – "esta creencia, las personas que tienen mucho dinero robaron y hacen trampa"

2 = Lado del ojo – "esta creencia, las personas que tienen mucho dinero robaron y hacen trampa"

3 = Debajo del ojo – "esta creencia, las personas que tienen mucho dinero robaron y hacen trampa"

4 = Debajo de la nariz – "esta creencia, las personas que tienen mucho dinero robaron y hacen trampa"

5 = Debajo de la boca – "esta creencia, las personas que tienen mucho dinero robaron y hacen trampa"

6 = Clavícula – "esta creencia, las personas que tienen mucho dinero robaron y hacen trampa"

7 = Debajo del brazo – "esta creencia, las personas que tienen mucho dinero robaron y hacen trampa"

8 = Sobre la cabeza – "esta creencia las personas que tienen mucho dinero robaron y hacen trampa"

Respiramos profundamente. Cuando terminamos, medimos la intensidad. ¿Sigue usted pensando que " Las personas que tienen mucho dinero es porque robaron y hacen trampa "? Repita en voz alta: "Las personas que tienen mucho dinero es porque robaron y hacen trampa". Si la intensidad no ha bajado a cero continuamos tapeando. Y así sucesivamente seguimos midiendo la intensidad hasta que llegue a cero.

Mientras tapeamos esta creencia seguramente surgiran otras creencias o imagines o recuerdos con respecto al poder. Debe por lo tanto tapear con todo esto .

Escriba a continuación todos los pensamientos e imágnes que surjan mientras tapea:

1 -

2 -

3 -

4 -

5 -

6 -

7 -

8 -

9 -

10 –

El dinero es sucio y es la causa de todo lo malo

Esta es una creencia muy popular que ha sido transmitida de genereación en generación. Yo recuerdo que mi padre siempre me decía antes de comer:" Andá a lavarte las manos porque tocaste dinero".

Si pensamos que el dinero es sucio no vamos a querer estar cerca de él. Tenemos inconcientemente el miedo de que porque es sucio nos va transmitir alguna enfermadad o nos va dañar de alguna manera. Si usted se pone a pensar cuando sale a la calle no sólo toca dinero sinó que papeles, ropa , se sienta en un aciento donde alguien más se ha sentado , etc etc y no está preocupado de que debe lavarse las manos cada vez que toca un libro, papel , ropa en una tienda, etc.

Con respecto a la creencia de que el dinero es la raíz de todo lo malo, por supuesto que exiten muchas personas que están dispuestas a hacer cosas malas con el dinero. Pero eso no significa que el dinero es la raiz de todo lo malo. La persona utiliza en este caso el dinero en forma negativa. Creo que ésta es una generalización my grave. Es también una manera cómoda de seguir protestando y envidiando a los que tienen mucho dinero.

Gracias al dinero se han hecho cosas extraordinarias. La Madre Teresa de Calcuta realizó grandezas gracias al dinero.

1) El dinero es sucio y la causa de todo lo malo

Repita la siguiente frase tres veces mientras tapea en el punto de karate:

"Aunque yo creo que el dinero es sucio y es la causa de todo lo malo, yo profunda y completamente me amo y me acepto a mi misma"

1 = Lado de la ceja – "esta creencia, el dinero es sucio y es la causa de todo lo malo"

2 = Lado del ojo – "esta creencia, el dinero es sucio y es la causa de todo lo malo"

3 = Debajo del ojo – "esta creencia, el dinero es sucio y es la causa de todo lo malo"

4 = Debajo de la nariz – "esta creencia, el dinero es sucio y es la causa de todo lo malo"

5 = Debajo de la boca – "esta creencia, el dinero es sucio y es la causa de todo lo malo"

6 = Clavícula – "esta creencia, el dinero es sucio y es la causa de todo lo malo"

7 = Debajo del brazo – "esta creencia, el dinero es sucio y es la causa de todo lo malo"

8 = Sobre la cabeza – "esta creencia, el dinero es sucio es la causa de todo lo malo".

Respiramos profundamente. Cuando terminamos, medimos la intensidad. ¿Sigue usted pensando que " El dinero es sucio y es la causa de todo lo malo "?

Repita en voz alta: "El dinero es sucio y es la causa de todo lomalo". Si la intensidad no ha bajado a cero continuamos tapeando. Y así sucesivamente seguimos midiendo la intensidad hasta que llegue a cero.

Mientras tapeamos esta creencia seguramente surgiran otras creencias o imagines o recuerdos con respecto al poder. Debe por lo tanto tapear con todo esto.

Escriba a continuación todos los pensamientos e imágnes que surjan mientras tapea:

1 -
2 -
3 -
4 -
5 -
6 -
7 -
8 -
9 -
10 -

Es mejor dar que recibir

"Por cada persona que da, deber haber alguien que recibe. Por cada persona que recibe, debe haber alguien que da. Harv Eker.

Muchos de nostros fuimos educados con la creencia que es mejor dar que recibir. El dar y recibir es un balance. No podemos dar y dar y nunca recibir nada, asi como tampoco podemos recibir y recibir y nunca dar nada.

Dar es una cosa buena pero no hay nada de malo en recibir. El no querer recibir no lo va a hacer una mejor persona. Si usted se siente incómodo recibiendo dinero o cosas, usted buscará maneras inconcientes de no aceptar ya sea dinero, regalos o más ingresos. Seguramente evitará participar en oportunidades financieras que dan algo valiososo a los demás para evitar recibir.

Creo que debemos comenzar a comprender la diferencia entre egoismo (satisfascer nuestras necesidades a expensas de los demás) y cuidarnos a nostros mismos pero no a costa de los demás.
Recuerde que no podemos dar lo que no tenemos. Como va a dar si no recibe nada?, esta idea errónea ha llevado a muchos a no aceptar de los demás.
Muchas personas quieren darnos y si no lo aceptamos la persona en cuestión se sentirá rechazada.

El punto acá es que no es mejor dar ni es mejor recibir. Es mejor dar y recibir. De esta manera vamos a crear un balance en nuestra vida. En la vida compartimos constantemente si no recibimos no tenemos nada para dar.

1) Es mejor dar que recibir

Repita la siguiente frase tres veces mientras tapea en el punto de karate:

"Aunque yo creo que es mejor dar que recibir, yo profunda y completamente me amo y me acepto a mi misma"

1 = Lado de la ceja – "esta creencia, es mejor dar que recibir"

2 = Lado del ojo – "esta creencia, es mejor dar que recibir"

3 = Debajo del ojo – "esta creencia, es mejor dar que recibir"

4 = Debajo de la nariz – "esta creencia, es mejor dar que recibir"

5 = Debajo de la boca – "esta creencia, es mejor dar que recibir"

6 = Clavícula – "esta creencia, es mejor dar que recibir"

7 = Debajo del brazo – "esta creencia, es mejor dar que recibir"

8 = Sobre la cabeza – "esta creencia, es mejor dar que recibir".

Respiramos profundamente. Cuando terminamos, medimos la intensidad. ¿Sigue usted pensando que " Es mejor dar que reicibir "? Repita en voz alta: "Es mejor dar que recibir". Si la intensidad no ha bajado a cero continuamos tapeando. Y así sucesivamente seguimos midiendo la intensidad hasta que llegue a cero.

Mientras tapeamos esta creencia seguramente surgiran otras creencias o imagines o recuerdos con respecto al poder. Debe por lo tanto tapear con todo esto.

Escriba a continuación todos los pensamientos e imágnes que surjan mientras tapea:

1 -

2 -

3 -

4 -

5 -

6 -

7 -

8 -

9 -

10 -

Capítulo 5 : "Mas creencias que nos bloquean"

Hasta ahora nos hemos enfocado en las creencias más populares sobre el dinero que estan impregnadas en el incociente colectivo. Una vez que usted pueda resolver estos conflictos y liberar estas creencias negativas que he descripto en los capítulos anteriores, se sentirá más abierto y dispuesto ha encontrar otras creencias limitantes que ha adquirido desde su nacimiento.

Como dije anteriormente el tema de las creencias sobre el dinero y la relación que tenemos con el mismo involucra creencias muy personales porque cada uno de nostros ha nacido en familias diferentes, paises diferentes y ha tenido experiencias diferentes.

Para poder ayudarlo a seguir eliminando creencias que no lo dejan recibir abundancia y prosperidad de dinero me gustaría mostrarle otras creencias y pensamientos que son universales y lo ayudarán a encontrar la raiz de muchos de sus problemas de dinero.

Mas creencias:

1. El dinero no es importante
2. Para ser bueno debo ser pobre
3. Si tengo mas dinero que otros, ellos no tendrán suficiente

4. Para tener mucho dinero debo trabajar duro y sacrificar muchas cosas
5. El Diablo es el que quiere mucho dinero, debo ser humilde y no esperar ninguna recompensa por mis esfuerzos
6. Los que tienen mucho dinero lo hicieron a expensas de los demás.
7. Hay que ahorrar dinero por si algo malo sucede.
8. Esta bien gastar dinero para mi familia pero si lo hago para mi soy egoista.
9. No merezco tener mucho dinero
10. El dinero escasea
11. Ha que nacer con dinero para ser rico
12. Mi familia y amigos me van a rechazar si tengo mucho dinero
13. Las personas espirituales no les importa el dinero
14. Se necesita dinero para hacer mas dinero
15. Nunca tengo suficiente dinero
16. Nunca puedo tener lo que quiero
17. No merezco ser feliz y exitoso
18. Necesito que alguien me salve de mi situation financiera
19. Si tengo mucho dinero traicionaré a mi padre que nunca lo tuvo.
20. Tener mucho dinero complica tu vida

Creencia: El dinero no es importante

Si usted cree que el dinero no es importante nunca tendrá dinero. Las personas ricas entienden la importancia del dinero y el lugar del mismo en la sociedad. Las personas que piensan que el dinero no es importante generalmente dicen: " El dinero no es tan imporatnte como el amor". Considera usted que su brazo es mas importante que su pierna?

Ambos son importantes, el dinero y el amor. El dinero es importante en las areas donde funciona y no es importante en las areas que no funciona. El amor es importantísimo porque es el fundamento de nuestras vidas. Pero no creo que usted podrá pagar sus cuentas con el amor y sin dinero.

Esta creencia de que el dinero no es importante es una consecuencia de otras creencias: el dinero es sucio, es mejor ser pobre que rico, si sos pobre te irás al cielo y muchas más.

El dinero es importante porque vivimos en una sociedad donde intercambiamos información, bienes, y cosas por dinero. Usted no sube a un colectivo y le da amor al chofer y lo deja subir. Usted paga su tarifa y sube al colectivo.

El dinero es importante cuando lo utilizamos correctamente. El dinero en si mismo no es malo , el uso que le damos puede ser malo o bueno.

En su libro "Acres de diamantes", Russell Conwell cuenta la siguiente historia:

"Y les digo a ustedes que deben volverse ricos y que es su deber ser ricos. Cuántos de ustedes me han dicho " Porque usted que es un Ministro Cristiano pierde el tiempo aconsejando a los jovenes a que se hagan ricos?".

No es eso terrible? Porque no enseña la Biblia ? Porque el hacerse rico honestamente es enseñar la Biblia. Esa es la razón.

Y porque gracias al dinero pudemos publicar la Biblia, construir nuestras iglesias, enviar misioneros a ayudar a los demás. Por eso usted debe hacerse rico. Es un gran error el creer que usted debe ser pobre para ser totalmente puro."

Es interesante, cuántos de nosotros hemos sido condicionados a creer que no podemos tener dinero y ser espirituales?.

1) El dinero no es importante

Repita la siguiente frase tres veces mientras tapea en el punto de karate:

"Aunque yo creo que el dinero no es imporante", yo profunda y completamente me acepto a mi mismo.

1 = Lado de la ceja – "esta creencia, el dinero no es importante"

2 = Lado del ojo – "esta creencia, el dinero no es importante"

3 = Debajo del ojo – "esta creencia, el dinero no es importante"

4 = Debajo de la nariz – "esta creencia, el dinero no es espiritual"

5 = Debajo de la boca – "esta creencia, el dinero no es espiritual"

6 = Clavícula – "esta creencia, el dinero no es espiritual"

7 = Debajo del brazo – "es mejor ser pobre que rico"

8 = Sobre la cabeza – "si soy pobre tendré Ganado el cielo".

1 = Lado de la ceja – "esto es lo que aprendi"

2 = Lado del ojo – "esto es lo que me enseñaron"

3 = Debajo del ojo – "toda mi vida me dijeron que el dinero no es imporante"

4 = Debajo de la nariz – "que el dinero es sucio"

5 = Debajo de la boca – "que tener dinero me va a convertir en una persona mala"

6 = Clavícula – "que no puedo ser espiritual y tener mucho dinero"

7 = Debajo del brazo – "esta confusión"

8 = Sobre la cabeza – "como voy a pagar mis cuentas sin dinero?".

1 = Lado de la ceja – "como voy a vestirme y comer sin dinero?"

2 = Lado del ojo – "pero si tengo mucho dinero me voy a condenar"

3 = Debajo del ojo – "es mas importante el amor que el dinero"

4 = Debajo de la nariz – "que es mas importante?"

5 = Debajo de la boca – "porque no puedo tener dinero y amor?"

6 = Clavícula – "es que me dijeron que si tengo amor no tengo dinero?"

7 = Debajo del brazo – "seguro que si tengo dinero no tengo amor"

8 = Sobre la cabeza – "yo quiero tener amor".

1 = Lado de la ceja – "por eso no me interesa el dinero"

2 = Lado del ojo – "el dinero no es importante"

3 = Debajo del ojo – "pero como puedo vivir descentemente sin dinero?"

4 = Debajo de la nariz – "esta confusión"

5 = Debajo de la boca – "yo quiero tener dinero"

6 = Clavícula – "pero tengo miedo de no ser espiritual"

7 = Debajo del brazo – "este miedo, si tengo dinero no soy espiritual"

8 = Sobre la cabeza – "este miedo, si tengo dinero no tengo amor".

1 = Lado de la ceja – "pero ahora entiendo"

2 = Lado del ojo – "que el dinero es importante asi como lo es el amor"

3 = Debajo del ojo – "si yo soy Buena persona el dinero no me va a corromper"

4 = Debajo de la nariz – "con mucho dinero puedo hacer muchas cosas"

5 = Debajo de la boca – "puedo ayudar a los demas"

6 = Clavícula – "puedo hacer feliz a mis seres queridos"

7 = Debajo del brazo – "entonces tal vez el problema no es el dinero"

8 = Sobre la cabeza – "el problema es mi miedo".

1 = Lado de la ceja – "este miedo de que si tengo dinero voy a ser corrupto"

2 = Lado del ojo – "este miedo de que si tengo dinero me voy a condenar"

3 = Debajo del ojo – "este miedo de que si tengo dinero no voy a ser feliz en el amor"

4 = Debajo de la nariz – "todos estos miedos"

5 = Debajo de la boca – "yo elijo ahora comprender"

6 = Clavícula – "que el problema no es el dinero"

7 = Debajo del brazo – "el problema es que no confio en mi mismo"

8 = Sobre la cabeza – "que no creo que soy una Buena persona".

1 = Lado de la ceja – "por eso ahora elijo"

2 = Lado del ojo – "confiar en mi"

3 = Debajo del ojo – "liberar mi necesidad de no tener dinero"

4 = Debajo de la nariz – "confiar que con mi dinero podre ayudar a muchos"

5 = Debajo de la boca – "entender que el dinero es importante"

6 = Clavícula – "entender que el dinero es espiritual"

7 = Debajo del brazo – "porque Dios es abundancia"

8 = Sobre la cabeza – "elijo ahora confiar en mi, sabiendo que el dinero no me va a corromper porque soy una excelente persona. Gracias Dios por hacerme tomar conciencia de esto.

Respiramos profundamente. Cuando terminamos, medimos la intensidad. ¿Sigue usted pensando que " El dinero no es importante "? Repita en voz alta: "El dinero no es importante". Si la intensidad no ha bajado a cero continuamos tapeando. Y así sucesivamente seguimos midiendo la intensidad hasta que llegue a cero.

Mientras tapeamos esta creencia seguramente surgiran otras creencias o imagines o recuerdos con respecto al poder. Debe por lo tanto tapear con todo esto . Escriba a continuación todos los pensamientos e imágnes que surjan mientras tapea:

1 -

2 -

3 -

4 -

5 -

6 -

7 -

8 -

2) Para ser bueno debo ser pobre

Repita la siguiente frase tres veces mientras tapea en el punto de karate:

"Aunque yo creo que para ser una buena persona debo ser pobre, yo profunda y completamente me amo y me acepto a mi mismo.

1 = Lado de la ceja – "esta creencia, para ser bueno debo ser pobre"

2 = Lado del ojo – "esta creencia, para ser bueno debo ser pobre"

3 = Debajo del ojo – "esta creencia, para ser bueno debo ser pobre"

4 = Debajo de la nariz – "esta creencia, para ser bueno debo ser pobre"

5 = Debajo de la boca – "esta creencia, para ser bueno debo ser pobre"

6 = Clavícula – "esta creencia, para ser bueno debo ser pobre"

7 = Debajo del brazo – "esta creencia, para ser bueno debo ser pobre"

8 = Sobre la cabeza – "esta creencia, para ser bueno debo ser pobre".

Respiramos profundamente. Cuando terminamos, medimos la intensidad. ¿Sigue usted pensando que " Para ser bueno debo ser pobre "? Repita en voz alta: "Para ser bueno debo ser pobre". Si la intensidad no ha bajado a cero continuamos tapeando. Y así

sucesivamente seguimos midiendo la intensidad hasta que llegue a cero.

Mientras tapeamos esta creencia seguramente surgiran otras creencias o imagines o recuerdos con respecto al poder. Debe por lo tanto tapear con todo esto.

Escriba a continuación todos los pensamientos e imágnes que surjan mientras tapea:

1 -

2 -

3 -

4 -

5 -

6 -

7 -

8 -

9 -

10 -

3) Si tengo mas dinero que otros, ellos no tendrán suficiente

Repita la siguiente frase tres veces mientras tapea en el punto de karate:

"Aunque yo creo que si tengo mas dinero que otros, ellos no tendrán suficiente, yo profunda y completamente me amo y me acepto a mi mismo."

1 = Lado de la ceja – "esta creencia, si tengo mas dinero que otros, ellos no tendrán suficiente"

2 = Lado del ojo – "esta creencia, si tengo mas dinero que otros, ellos no tendrán suficiente"

3 = Debajo del ojo – "esta creencia, si tengo mas dinero que otros, ellos no tendrán suficiente"

4 = Debajo de la nariz – "esta creencia, si tengo mas dinero que otros, ellos no tendrán suficiente"

5 = Debajo de la boca – "esta creencia, si tengo mas dinero que otros, ellos no tendrán suficiente"

6 = Clavícula – "esta creencia, si tengo mas dinero que otros, ellos no tendrán suficiente"

7 = Debajo del brazo – "esta creencia, si tengo mas dinero que otros, ellos no tendrán suficiente"

8 = Sobre la cabeza – "esta creencia, si tengo mas dinero que otros, ellos no tendrán suficiente".

Respiramos profundamente. Cuando terminamos, medimos la intensidad. ¿Sigue usted pensando que " Si tengo mas dinero que otros, ellos no tendrán suficiente "? Repita en voz alta: "Si tengo mas dinero que otros , ellos no tendrán suficiente". Si la intensidad no ha bajado a cero continuamos tapeando. Y así sucesivamente seguimos midiendo la intensidad hasta que llegue a cero.

Mientras tapeamos esta creencia seguramente surgiran otras creencias o imagines o recuerdos con respecto al poder. Debe por lo tanto tapear con todo esto.

Escriba a continuación todos los pensamientos e imágnes que surjan mientras tapea:

1 -
2 -
3 -
4 -
5 -
6 -
7 -
8 -
9 -
10 -

4) Para tener mucho dinero debo trabajar duro y sacrificar muchas cosas

Repita la siguiente frase tres veces mientras tapea en el punto de karate:

"Aunque yo creo que para tener mucho dinero debo trabajar duro y sacrificar muchas cosas", yo profundamente me acepto a mi mismo.

1 = Lado de la ceja – "esta creencia, para tener mucho dinero debo trabajar duro y sacrificar muchas cosas"

2 = Lado del ojo – "esta creencia, para tener mucho dinero debo trabajar duro y sacrificar muchas cosas"

3 = Debajo del ojo – "esta creencia, para tener mucho dinero debo trabajar duro y sacrificar muchas cosas"

4 = Debajo de la nariz – "esta creencia, para tener mucho dinero debo trabajar duro y sacrificar muchas cosas"

5 = Debajo de la boca – "esta creencia, para tener mucho dinero debo trabajar duro y sacrificar muchas cosas"

6 = Clavícula – "esta creencia, para tener mucho dinero debo trabajar duro y sacrificar muchas cosas"

7 = Debajo del brazo – "esta creencia, para tener mucho dinero debo trabajar duro y sacrificar muchas cosas"

8 = Sobre la cabeza – "esta creencia, para tener mucho dinero debo trabajar duro y sacrificar muchas cosas".

Respiramos profundamente. Cuando terminamos, medimos la intensidad. ¿Sigue usted pensando que " Para tener mucho dinero debo trabajar duro y sacrificar muchas cosas "? Repita en voz alta: "Para tener mucho dinero debo trabajar duro y sacrificar muchas cosas". Si la intensidad no ha bajado a cero continuamos tapeando. Y así sucesivamente seguimos midiendo la intensidad hasta que llegue a cero.

Mientras tapeamos esta creencia seguramente surgiran otras creencias o imagines o recuerdos con respecto al poder. Debe por lo tanto tapear con todo esto .

Escriba a continuación todos los pensamientos e imágnes que surjan mientras tapea:

1 -

2 -

3 -

4 -

5 -

6 -

7 -

8 -

9 -

10 -

5) Debo ser humilde y no esperar ninguna recompensa por mis esfuerzos

Repita la siguiente frase tres veces mientras tapea en el punto de karate:

"Aunque yo creo que debo ser humilde y no esperar ninguna recompensa por mis esfuerzos", yo profundamente me acepto a mi mismo.

1 = Lado de la ceja – "esta creencia, debo ser humilde y no esperar ninguna recompensa por mis esfuerzos"

2 = Lado del ojo – "esta creencia, debo ser humilde y no esperar ninguna recompensa por mis esfuerzos"

3 = Debajo del ojo – "esta creencia, debo ser humilde y no esperar ninguna recompensa por mis esfuerzos"

4 = Debajo de la nariz – "esta creencia, , debo ser humilde y no esperar ninguna recompensa por mis esfuerzos"

5 = Debajo de la boca – "esta creencia, , debo ser humilde y no esperar ninguna recompensa por mis esfuerzos"

6 = Clavícula – "esta creencia, , debo ser humilde y no esperar ninguna recompensa por mis esfuerzos"

7 = Debajo del brazo – "esta creencia, , debo ser humilde y no esperar ninguna recompensa por mis esfuerzos"

8 = Sobre la cabeza – "esta creencia, , debo ser humilde y no esperar ninguna recompensa por mis esfuerzos".

Respiramos profundamente. Cuando terminamos, medimos la intensidad. ¿Sigue usted pensando que ", debo ser humilde y no esperar ninguna recompensa por mis esfuerzos "? Repita en voz alta: ", debo ser humilde y no esperar ninguna recompensa por mis esfuerzos". Si la intensidad no ha bajado a cero continuamos tapeando. Y así sucesivamente seguimos midiendo la intensidad hasta que llegue a cero.

Mientras tapeamos esta creencia seguramente surgiran otras creencias o imagines o recuerdos con respecto al poder. Debe por lo tanto tapear con todo esto.

Escriba a continuación todos los pensamientos e imágnes que surjan mientras tapea:

1 -

2 -

3 -

4 -

5 -

6 -

7 -

8 -

9 -

10 –

6) Los que tienen mucho dinero lo hicieron a expensas de los demás

Repita la siguiente frase tres veces mientras tapea en el punto de karate:

"Aunque yo creo que los que tienen mucho dinero lo hicieron a expensas de los demás", yo profundamente me acepto a mi mismo.

1 = Lado de la ceja – "esta creencia, los que tienen mucho dinero lo hicieron a expensas de los demás"

2 = Lado del ojo – "esta creencia, los que tienen mucho dinero lo hicieron a expensas de los demás"

3 = Debajo del ojo – "esta creencia, los que tienen mucho dinero lo hicieron a expensas de los demás"

4 = Debajo de la nariz – "esta creencia, los que tienen mucho dinero lo hicieron a expensas de los demás"

5 = Debajo de la boca – "esta creencia, los que tienen mucho dinero lo hicieron a expensas de los demás"

6 = Clavícula – "esta creencia, los que tienen mucho dinero lo hicieron a expensas de los demás"

7 = Debajo del brazo – "esta creencia, los que tienen mucho dinero lo hicieron a expensas de los demás"

8 = Sobre la cabeza – "esta creencia, los que tienen mucho dinero lo hicieron a expensas de los demás".

Respiramos profundamente. Cuando terminamos, medimos la intensidad. ¿Sigue usted pensando que " Los que tienen mucho dinero lo hicieron a expensas de los demás "? Repita en voz alta: "Los que tienen mucho dinero lo hicieron a expensas de los demás". Si la intensidad no ha bajado a cero continuamos tapeando. Y así sucesivamente seguimos midiendo la intensidad hasta que llegue a cero.

Mientras tapeamos esta creencia seguramente surgiran otras creencias o imagines o recuerdos con respecto al poder. Debe por lo tanto tapear con todo esto.

Escriba a continuación todos los pensamientos e imágnes que surjan mientras tapea:

1 -
2 -
3 -
4 -
5 -
6 -
7 -
8 -
9 -
10 -

7) Hay que ahorrar dinero por si algo malo sucede

Repita la siguiente frase tres veces mientras tapea en el punto de karate:

"Aunque yo creo que hay que ahorrar dinero por si algo malo sucede", yo profunda y completamente me amo y me acepto a mi mismo.

1 = Lado de la ceja – "esta creencia, hay que ahorrar dinero por si algo malo sucede"

2 = Lado del ojo – "esta creencia, hay que ahorrar dinero por si algo malo sucede"

3 = Debajo del ojo – "esta creencia, hay que ahorrar dinero por si algo malo sucede"

4 = Debajo de la nariz – "esta creencia, hay que ahorrar dinero por si algo malo sucede"

5 = Debajo de la boca – "esta creencia, hay que ahorrar dinero por si algo malo sucede"

6 = Clavícula – "esta creencia, hay que ahorrar dinero por si algo malo sucede"

7 = Debajo del brazo – "esta creencia, hay que ahorrar dinero por si algo malo sucede"

8 = Sobre la cabeza – "esta creencia, hay que ahorrar dinero por si algo malo sucede".

Respiramos profundamente. Cuando terminamos, medimos la intensidad. ¿Sigue usted pensando que " Hay que ahorrar dinero por si algo malo sucede "? Repita en voz alta: "Hay que ahorrar dinero por si algo malo sucede". Si la intensidad no ha bajado a cero continuamos tapeando. Y así sucesivamente seguimos midiendo la intensidad hasta que llegue a cero.

Mientras tapeamos esta creencia seguramente surgiran otras creencias o imagines o recuerdos con respecto al poder. Debe por lo tanto tapear con todo esto.

Escriba a continuación todos los pensamientos e imágnes que surjan mientras tapea:

1 -

2 -

3 -

4 -

5 -

6 -

7 -

8 -

9 -

10 -

8) Esta bien gastar dinero para mi familia pero si lo hago para mi soy egoista

Repita la siguiente frase tres veces mientras tapea en el punto de karate:

"Aunque yo creo que esta bien gastar dinero para mi familia pero si lo hago para mi soy egoista", yo profundamente me acepto a mi mismo.

1 = Lado de la ceja – "esta creencia, esta bien gastar dinero para mi familia, si lo hago para mi soy egoista"

2 = Lado del ojo – "esta creencia, esta bien gastar dinero para mi familia, si lo hago para mi soy egoista"

3 = Debajo del ojo – "esta creencia, esta bien gastar dinero para mi familia, si lo hago para mi soy egoista"

4 = Debajo de la nariz – "esta creencia, esta bien gastar dinero para mi familia, si lo hago para mi soy egoista"

5 = Debajo de la boca – "esta creencia, esta bien gastar dinero para mi familia, si lo hago para mi soy egoista"

6 = Clavícula – "esta creencia, esta bien gastar dinero para mi familia, si lo hago para mi soy egoista"

7 = Debajo del brazo – "esta creencia, esta bien gastar dinero para mi familia, si lo hago para mi soy egoista"

8 = Sobre la cabeza – "esta creencia, esta bien gastar dinero para mi familia, si lo hago para mi soy egoista".

Respiramos profundamente. Cuando terminamos, medimos la intensidad. ¿Sigue usted pensando que "

Esta bien gastar dinero para mi familia pero si lo hago para mi soy egoista "? Repita en voz alta: "Esta bien gastar dinero para mi familia pero si lo hago para mi soy egoista". Si la intensidad no ha bajado a cero continuamos tapeando. Y así sucesivamente seguimos midiendo la intensidad hasta que llegue a cero.

Mientras tapeamos esta creencia seguramente surgiran otras creencias o imagines o recuerdos con respecto al poder. Debe por lo tanto tapear con todo esto.

Escriba a continuación todos los pensamientos e imágnes que surjan mientras tapea:

1 -
2 -
3 -
4 -
5 -
6 -
7 -
8 -
9 -
10 -

9) Secuencia de tapeo para la creencia: No merezco tener mucho dinero

Repita la siguiente frase tres veces mientras tapea en el punto de karate:

"Aunque yo creo que no merezco tener mucho dinero", yo profundamente me acepto a mi mismo.

1 = Lado de la ceja – "esta creencia, no merezco tener mucho dinero"

2 = Lado del ojo – "esta creencia, no merezco tener mucho dinero"

3 = Debajo del ojo – "esta creencia no merezco tener mucho dinero"

4 = Debajo de la nariz – "esta creencia, no merezco tener mucho dinero"

5 = Debajo de la boca – "esta creencia, no merezco tener mucho dinero"

6 = Clavícula – "esta creencia, no merezco tener mucho dinero"

7 = Debajo del brazo – "esta creencia, no merezco tener mucho dinero"

8 = Sobre la cabeza – "esta creencia, no merezco tener mucho dinero".

Respiramos profundamente. Cuando terminamos, medimos la intensidad. ¿Sigue usted pensando que " no merezco tener mucho dinero "? Repita en voz alta: "no merezco tener mucho dinero". Si la intensidad no ha bajado a cero continuamos tapeando. Y así

sucesivamente seguimos midiendo la intensidad hasta que llegue a cero.

Mientras tapeamos esta creencia seguramente surgiran otras creencias o imagines o recuerdos con respecto al poder. Debe por lo tanto tapear con todo esto .

Escriba a continuación todos los pensamientos e imágnes que surjan mientras tapea:

1 -

2 -

3 -

4 -

5 -

6 -

7 -

8 -

9 -

10 -

10) El dinero escasea

Repita la siguiente frase tres veces mientras tapea en el punto de karate:

"Aunque yo creo que el dinero escasea, yo profunda y completamente me amo y me acepto a mi mismo.

1 = Lado de la ceja – "esta creencia, el dinero escasea"

2 = Lado del ojo – "esta creencia, el dinero escasea"

3 = Debajo del ojo – "esta creencia el dinero escasea"

4 = Debajo de la nariz – "esta creencia, el dinero escasea"

5 = Debajo de la boca – "esta creencia, el dinero escasea"

6 = Clavícula – "esta creencia, el dinero escasea"

7 = Debajo del brazo – "esta creencia el dinero escasea"

8 = Sobre la cabeza – "esta creencia, el dinero escasea".

Respiramos profundamente. Cuando terminamos, medimos la intensidad. ¿Sigue usted pensando que "El dinero escasea "? Repita en voz alta: "el dinero escasea". Si la intensidad no ha bajado a cero continuamos tapeando. Y así sucesivamente seguimos midiendo la intensidad hasta que llegue a cero.

Mientras tapeamos esta creencia seguramente surgiran otras creencias o imagines o recuerdos con respecto al poder. Debe por lo tanto tapear con todo esto .

Escriba a continuación todos los pensamientos e imágnes que surjan mientras tapea:

1 -

2 -

3 -

4 -

5 -

6 -

7 -

8 -

9 -

10 -

11) Hay que nacer con dinero para ser rico

Repita la siguiente frase tres veces mientras tapea en el punto de karate:

"Aunque yo creo hay que nacer con dinero para ser rico", yo profundamente me acepto a mi mismo.

1 = Lado de la ceja – "esta creencia, creo hay que nacer con dinero para ser rico"

2 = Lado del ojo – "esta creencia, creo hay que nacer con dinero para ser rico"

3 = Debajo del ojo – "esta creencia creo hay que nacer con dinero para ser rico"

4 = Debajo de la nariz – "esta creencia, creo hay que nacer con dinero para ser rico"

5 = Debajo de la boca – "esta creencia, creo hay que nacer con dinero para ser rico"

6 = Clavícula – "esta creencia, creo hay que nacer con dinero para ser rico"

7 = Debajo del brazo – "esta creencia creo hay que nacer con dinero para ser rico"

8 = Sobre la cabeza – "esta creencia, creo hay que nacer con dinero para ser rico".

Respiramos profundamente. Cuando terminamos, medimos la intensidad. ¿Sigue usted pensando que "Hay que nacer con dinero para ser rico "? Repita en voz alta: "Hay que nacer con dinero para ser rico". Si la intensidad no ha bajado a cero continuamos tapeando. Y así sucesivamente seguimos midiendo la intensidad hasta que llegue a cero.

Mientras tapeamos esta creencia seguramente surgiran otras creencias o imagines o recuerdos con respecto al poder. Debe por lo tanto tapear con todo esto .

Escriba a continuación todos los pensamientos e imágnes que surjan mientras tapea:

1 -

2 -

3 -

4 -

5 -

6 -

7 -

8 -

9 -

10 -

12) Mi familia y amigos me van a rechazar si tengo mucho dinero

Repita la siguiente frase tres veces mientras tapea en el punto de karate:

"Aunque yo creo mi familia y amigos me van a rechazar si tengo mucho dinero", yo profundamente me acepto a mi mismo.

1 = Lado de la ceja – "esta creencia, mi familia y amigos me van a rechazar si tengo mucho dinero"

2 = Lado del ojo – "esta creencia, mi familia y amigos me van a rechazar si tengo mucho dinero"

3 = Debajo del ojo – "esta creencia mi familia y amigos me van a rechazar si tengo mucho dinero"

4 = Debajo de la nariz – "esta creencia, mi familia y amigos me van a rechazar si tengo mucho dinero"

5 = Debajo de la boca – "esta creencia, mi familia y amigos me van a rechazar si tengo mucho dinero"

6 = Clavícula – "esta creencia, mi familia y amigos me van a rechazar si tengo mucho dinero"

7 = Debajo del brazo – "esta creencia mi familia y amigos me van a rechazar si tengo mucho dinero"

8 = Sobre la cabeza – "esta creencia, mi familia y amigos me van a rechazar si tengo mucho dinero".

Respiramos profundamente. Cuando terminamos, medimos la intensidad. ¿Sigue usted pensando que "Mi familia y amigos me van a rechazar si tengo mucho dinero "? Repita en voz alta: "Mmi familia y amigos me van a rechazar si tengo mucho dinero". Si la intensidad no ha bajado a cero continuamos tapeando. Y así sucesivamente seguimos midiendo la intensidad hasta que llegue a cero.

Mientras tapeamos esta creencia seguramente surgiran otras creencias o imagines o recuerdos con respecto al poder. Debe por lo tanto tapear con todo esto .

Escriba a continuación todos los pensamientos e imágnes que surjan mientras tapea:

1 -

2 -

3 -

4 -

5 -

6 -

7 -

8 -

9 -

10 -

13) Las personas espirituales no les importa el dinero

Repita la siguiente frase tres veces mientras tapea en el punto de karate:

"Aunque yo creo a las personas espirituales no les importa el dinero", yo profundamente me acepto a mi mismo.

1 = Lado de la ceja – "esta creencia, a las personas espirituales no les importa el dinero"

2 = Lado del ojo – "esta creencia, a las personas espirituales no les importa el dinero"

3 = Debajo del ojo – "esta creencia a las personas espirituales no les importa el dinero"

4 = Debajo de la nariz – "esta creencia, a las personas espirituales no les importa el dinero"

5 = Debajo de la boca – "esta creencia, a las personas espirituales no les importa el dinero"

6 = Clavícula – "esta creencia, a las personas espirituales no les importa el dinero"

7 = Debajo del brazo – "esta creencia a las personas espirituales no les importa el dinero"

8 = Sobre la cabeza – "esta creencia, a las personas espirituales no les importa el dinero".

Respiramos profundamente. Cuando terminamos, medimos la intensidad. ¿Sigue usted pensando que "A las personas espirituales no les importa el dinero"? Repita en voz alta: "A las personas espirituales no les importa el dinero". Si la intensidad no ha bajado a cero continuamos tapeando. Y así sucesivamente seguimos midiendo la intensidad hasta que llegue a cero.

Mientras tapeamos esta creencia seguramente surgiran otras creencias o imagines o recuerdos con respecto al poder. Debe por lo tanto tapear con todo esto.

Escriba a continuación todos los pensamientos e imágnes que surjan mientras tapea:

1 -
2 -
3 -
4 -
5 -
6 -
7 -
8 -
9 -
10 -

14) Se necesita dinero para hacer mas dinero

Repita la siguiente frase tres veces mientras tapea en el punto de karate:

"Aunque yo creo que se necesita dinero para hacer mas dinero", yo profundamente me acepto a mi mismo.

1 = Lado de la ceja – "esta creencia, se necesita dinero para hacer mas dinero"

2 = Lado del ojo – "esta creencia, se necesita dinero para hacer mas dinero"

3 = Debajo del ojo – "esta creencia se necesita dinero para hacer mas dinero"

4 = Debajo de la nariz – "esta creencia se necesita dinero para hacer mas dinero"

5 = Debajo de la boca – "esta creencia, se necesita dinero para hacer mas dinero"

6 = Clavícula – "esta creencia se necesita dinero para hacer mas dinero"

7 = Debajo del brazo – "esta creencia se necesita dinero para hacer mas dinero"

8 = Sobre la cabeza – "esta creencia, se necesita dinero para hacer mas dinero".

Respiramos profundamente. Cuando terminamos, medimos la intensidad. ¿Sigue usted pensando que "Se necesita dinero para hacer mas dinero "? Repita en voz alta: "Se necesita dinero para hacer mas dinero". Si la intensidad no ha bajado a cero continuamos tapeando. Y así sucesivamente seguimos midiendo la intensidad hasta que llegue a cero.

Mientras tapeamos esta creencia seguramente surgiran otras creencias o imagines o recuerdos con respecto al poder. Debe por lo tanto tapear con todo esto.

Escriba a continuación todos los pensamientos e imágnes que surjan mientras tapea:

1 -

2 -

3 -

4 -

5 -

6 -

7 -

8 -

9 -

10 -

15) Nunca tengo suficiente dinero

Repita la siguiente frase tres veces mientras tapea en el punto de karate:

"Aunque nunca tengo suficiente dinero", yo profundamente me acepto a mi mismo.

1 = Lado de la ceja – "esta fustración, nunca tengo suficiente dinero"

2 = Lado del ojo – "esta fustración, nunca tengo suficiente dinero"

3 = Debajo del ojo – "esta fustración, nunca tengo suficiente dinero"

4 = Debajo de la nariz – "esta fustración, nunca tengo suficiente dinero"

5 = Debajo de la boca – "esta fustración, nunca tengo suficiente dinero"

6 = Clavícula – "esta fustración, nunca tengo suficiente dinero"

7 = Debajo del brazo – "esta fustración, nunca tengo suficiente dinero"

8 = Sobre la cabeza – "esta fustración, nunca tengo suficiente dinero".

Respiramos profundamente. Cuando terminamos, medimos la intensidad. ¿Sigue usted pensando que "Nunca tengo suficiente dinero "? Repita en voz alta: "Nunca tengo suficiente dinero". Si la intensidad no ha bajado a cero continuamos tapeando. Y así sucesivamente seguimos midiendo la intensidad hasta que llegue a cero.

Mientras tapeamos esta creencia seguramente surgiran otras creencias o imagines o recuerdos con respecto al poder. Debe por lo tanto tapear con todo esto.

Escriba a continuación todos los pensamientos e imágnes que surjan mientras tapea:

1 -

2 -

3 -

4 -

5 -

6 -

7 -

8 -

9 -

10 -

16) Nunca puedo tener lo que quiero

Repita la siguiente frase tres veces mientras tapea en el punto de karate:

"Aunque nunca puedo tener lo que quiero", yo profundamente me acepto a mi mismo.

1 = Lado de la ceja – "esta creencia, nunca puedo tener lo que quiero"

2 = Lado del ojo – "esta creencia, nunca puedo tener lo que quiero"

3 = Debajo del ojo – "esta creencia, nunca puedo tener lo que quiero"

4 = Debajo de la nariz – "esta creencia, nunca puedo tener lo que quiero"

5 = Debajo de la boca – "esta creencia, nunca puedo tener lo que quiero"

6 = Clavícula – "esta creencia, nunca puedo tener lo que quiero"

7 = Debajo del brazo – "esta creencia, nunca puedo tener lo que quiero"

8 = Sobre la cabeza – "esta creencia, nunca puedo tener lo que quiero".

Respiramos profundamente. Cuando terminamos, medimos la intensidad. ¿Sigue usted pensando que "esta creencia, nunca puedo tener lo que quiero "? Repita en voz alta: "esta creencia, nunca puedo tener lo que quiero". Si la intensidad no ha bajado a cero continuamos tapeando. Y así sucesivamente seguimos midiendo la intensidad hasta que llegue a cero.

Mientras tapeamos esta creencia seguramente surgiran otras creencias o imagines o recuerdos con respecto al poder. Debe por lo tanto tapear con todo esto .

Escriba a continuación todos los pensamientos e imágnes que surjan mientras tapea:

1 -

2 -

3 -

4 -

5 -

6 -

7 -

8 -

9 -

10 -

17) No merezco ser feliz y exitoso

Repita la siguiente frase tres veces mientras tapea en el punto de karate:

"Aunque nunca yo creo que no merezco ser feliz y exitoso", yo profundamente me acepto a mi mismo.

1 = Lado de la ceja – "esta creencia, no merezco ser feliz y exitoso"

2 = Lado del ojo – "esta creencia, no merezco ser feliz y exitoso"

3 = Debajo del ojo – "esta creencia, no merezco ser feliz y exitoso"

4 = Debajo de la nariz – "esta creencia, no merezco ser feliz y exitoso"

5 = Debajo de la boca – "esta creencia, no merezco ser feliz y exitoso"

6 = Clavícula – "esta creencia, no merezco ser feliz y exitoso"

7 = Debajo del brazo – "esta creencia no merezco ser feliz y exitoso"

8 = Sobre la cabeza – "esta creencia, no merezco ser feliz y exitoso".

Respiramos profundamente. Cuando terminamos, medimos la intensidad. ¿Sigue usted pensando que "no merezco ser feliz y exitoso"? Repita en voz alta: "no merezco ser feliz y exitoso". Si la intensidad no ha bajado a cero continuamos tapeando. Y así sucesivamente seguimos midiendo la intensidad hasta que llegue a cero.

Mientras tapeamos esta creencia seguramente surgiran otras creencias o imagines o recuerdos con respecto al poder. Debe por lo tanto tapear con todo esto.

Escriba a continuación todos los pensamientos e imágnes que surjan mientras tapea:

1 -

2 -

3 -

4 -

5 -

6 -

7 -

8 -

9 -

10 -

18) Necesito que alguien me salve de mi situacion financiera

Repita la siguiente frase tres veces mientras tapea en el punto de karate:

"Aunque necesito que alguien me salve de mi situacion financiera", yo profundamente me acepto a mi mismo.

1 = Lado de la ceja – "esta impotencia, necesito que alguien me salve de mi situacion financiera"

2 = Lado del ojo – "esta impotencia, necesito que alguien me salve de mi situacion financiera"

3 = Debajo del ojo – "esta impotencia, necesito que alguien me salve de mi situacion financiera"

4 = Debajo de la nariz – "esta impotencia, necesito que alguien me salve de mi situacion financiera"

5 = Debajo de la boca – "esta impotencia, necesito que alguien me salve de mi situacion financiera"

6 = Clavícula – "esta impotencia, necesito que alguien me salve de mi situacion financiera"

7 = Debajo del brazo – "esta impotencia, necesito que alguien me salve de mi situacion financiera"

8 = Sobre la cabeza – "esta impotencia, necesito que alguien me salve de mi situacion financiera".

Respiramos profundamente. Cuando terminamos, medimos la intensidad. ¿Sigue usted pensando que "Necesito que alguien me salve de mi situacion financiera"? Repita en voz alta: "Necesito que alguien me salve de mi situacion financiera". Si la intensidad no ha bajado a cero continuamos tapeando. Y así

sucesivamente seguimos midiendo la intensidad hasta que llegue a cero.

Mientras tapeamos esta creencia seguramente surgiran otras creencias o imagines o recuerdos con respecto al poder. Debe por lo tanto tapear con todo esto.

Escriba a continuación todos los pensamientos e imágnes que surjan mientras tapea:

1 -
2 -
3 -
4 -
5 -
6 -
7 -
8 -
9 -
10 –

19) Secuencia de tapeo para la creencia: Si tengo mucho dinero traicionaré a mi padre que nunca lo tuvo

Repita la siguiente frase tres veces mientras tapea en el punto de karate:

"Aunque yo creo que si tengo mucho dinero traicionaré a mi padre que nunca lo tuvo", yo profundamente me acepto a mi mismo.

1 = Lado de la ceja – "este miedo, si tengo mucho dinero traicionaré a mi padre que nunca lo tuvo"

2 = Lado del ojo – "este miedo, si tengo mucho dinero traicionaré a mi padre que nunca lo tuvo"

3 = Debajo del ojo – "este miedo, si tengo mucho dinero traicionaré a mi padre que nunca lo tuvo"

4 = Debajo de la nariz – "este miedo, si tengo mucho dinero traicionaré a mi padre que nunca lo tuvo"

5 = Debajo de la boca – "este miedo, si tengo mucho dinero traicionaré a mi padre que nunca lo tuvo"

6 = Clavícula – "este miedo, si tengo mucho dinero traicionaré a mi padre que nunca lo tuvo"

7 = Debajo del brazo – "este miedo, si tengo mucho dinero traicionaré a mi padre que nunca lo tuvo"

8 = Sobre la cabeza – "este miedo, si tengo mucho dinero traicionaré a mi padre que nunca lo tuvo".

Respiramos profundamente. Cuando terminamos, medimos la intensidad. ¿Sigue usted pensando que "Si tengo mucho dinero traicionaré a mi padre que nunca lo tuvo "? Repita en voz alta: "Si tengo mucho dinero traicionaré a mi padre que nunca lo tuvo". Si la intensidad no ha bajado a cero continuamos tapeando. Y así sucesivamente seguimos midiendo la intensidad hasta que llegue a cero.

Mientras tapeamos esta creencia seguramente surgiran otras creencias o imagines o recuerdos con respecto al poder. Debe por lo tanto tapear con todo esto .

Escriba a continuación todos los pensamientos e imágnes que surjan mientras tapea:

1 -

2 -

3 -

4 -

5 -

6 -

7 -

8 -

9 -

10 -

20) Tener mucho dinero complica la vida

Repita la siguiente frase tres veces mientras tapea en el punto de karate:

"Aunque yo creo que tener mucho dinero complica la vida", yo profundamente me acepto a mi mismo.

1 = Lado de la ceja – "esta creencia, tener mucho dinero complica la vida"

2 = Lado del ojo – "esta creencia, tener mucho dinero complica la vida"

3 = Debajo del ojo – "esta creencia, tener mucho dinero complica la vida"

4 = Debajo de la nariz – "esta creencia, tener mucho dinero complica la vida"

5 = Debajo de la boca – "esta creencia, tener mucho dinero complica la vida"

6 = Clavícula – "esta creencia, tener mucho dinero complica la vida"

7 = Debajo del brazo – "esta creencia, tener mucho dinero complica la vida"

8 = Sobre la cabeza – "esta creencia, tener mucho dinero complica la vida".

Respiramos profundamente. Cuando terminamos, medimos la intensidad. ¿Sigue usted pensando que "Tener mucho dinero complica la vida "? Repita en voz alta: "Tener mucho dinero complica la vida". Si la intensidad no ha bajado a cero continuamos tapeando. Y así sucesivamente seguimos midiendo la intensidad hasta que llegue a cero.

Mientras tapeamos esta creencia seguramente surgiran otras creencias o imagines o recuerdos con respecto al poder. Debe por lo tanto tapear con todo esto.

Escriba a continuación todos los pensamientos e imágnes que surjan mientras tapea:

1 -
2 -
3 -
4 -
5 -
6 -
7 -
8 -
9 -
10 -

Conclusión

Que significa tener conciencia de prosperidad de dinero?
La prosperidad es un trabajo interior. Su conciencia de prosperidad de dinero es como usted piensa, cree y siente con respecto al dinero. Las personas que tienen una elevada conciencia de prosperidad de dinero saben que el dinero es ilimitado y están abierto a recibir dinero. Ellos confían en que sus necesidades serán satisfechas así como también sus deseos. Saben que hay suficiente dinero para todos por lo tanto dar, recibir y compartir dinero es un acto fácil de realizar para ellos.

Las personas que tienen conciencia de escasez con respecto al dinero nunca tienen suficiente dinero y tienen miedo de perder el poco que tienen. Se sienten necesitados e inadecuados. No confían que sus necesidades serán satisfechas, luchan constantemente y viven constantemente preocupados. Por lo tanto dar, recibir y compartir dinero es un conflicto para ellos.

La conciencia de prosperidad de dinero es un cambio de paradigma.

Bibliografia:

- Emotional Freedom Tecniques Manual. Introduction to EFT. Gary Cray. http://www.emofree.com
- You can heal your life. Louise Hay.

Otros libros por Carla Valencia

1. **Libro de Técnicas de liberación emocional : EFT Sanación emocional**

   Ejercicios prácticos. Una nueva forma para curar fobias, miedos, dolores físicos, depresión como también adelgazar, aumentar su autoestima y eliminar patrones que no lo dejan vivir en abundancia. http://www.autoayuda-eft.com/libro-de-tecnicas-de-liberacion-emocional-espanol.htm

2. **Cuaderno de ejercicios para aumentar la autoestima.**
   http://www.laautoesitma.com

3. **The Boost your Self esteem Workbook.**
   http://www.selfesteemawareness.com/workbook.htm

Acerca de Carla Valencia

La experiencia profesional de Carla incluye 15 años trabajando como Analista de Systemas y Escritor Técnico con Empresas de Exportación-Importación y Manufactureras. Su pasión acerca de los temas de autoestima la llevaron a escribir sus experiencias personales. Desde que ella era muy joven pasaba su tiempo investigando y entrevistando amigos y familiares sobre este tema de autoestima. Ella ha estado buscando diferentes alternativas para lidiar con este tema en diferentes niveles.

Ella estudió Metafisica, Budismo, EFT-CC (Basic EFT Certificate of Completion) y ha participado en varios workshops para trabajar en si misma. Ha estado usando diferentes ténicas desde hace mas de 10 años como ser Hoponopono, Técnicas de Liberación Emocional, Riberthing, Shadow Work y Meditación.

Carla publicó su primer libro cuando tenia 23 años, "Amémonos como Somos". Su pasión : "Dar su experiencia personal a los otros", su expresión: "Mi vida es mi enseñanza".

Autora de las siguientes Paginas Web:

http://www.selfesteemawareness.com

http://www.laautoestima.com

http://www.autoayuda-eft.com

http://www.frases-autoestima-autoayuda.com

http://www.las-emociones.com

Blog: http://eftfree.blogspot.com/

Made in the USA
Charleston, SC
16 December 2011

TURNING CURSES TO BLESSINGS

CARL L. FOX

Christian Faith International Ministries

Scripture quotations are from the King James Version of the Bible

Illustration used for cover design by:
Elaine Liberio
113A South St.
Gorham ME 04038

Published by Christian Faith International Ministries
412 Grape St.
Truth or Consequences NM 87901
505-894-5691
505-894-7474 (office)

ISBN: 0-9671353-1-1

Copyright © 1999 Christian Faith International
All rights reserved.

Fourth Printing

Printed in the United States by Morris Publishing
3212 East Highway 30
Kearney, NE 68847
1-800-650-7888

Dedication

I dedicate this book first of all, to my Father and my Lord Jesus Christ. Then I dedicate it to my wonderful wife, Sheila, who has been a great helpmate in life and ministry. Her prayers have broken down many barriers that needed to be overcome. Without those prayers, the book would never have been written.

Acknowledgements

My first thanks and heartfelt appreciation goes to Eli and Susanna Arvizu, who spent countless hours gathering copies of the classes I had taught, transcribing the classes from the tapes, sorting all the material, and continuing to spur on the vision of having the "Turning Curses to Blessings" class in a written format. Without their selfless service, we would not have been able to complete the manuscript.

Others who need to be thanked especially include, Elaine Liberio, for the God-inspired design of the book cover, Ed Johnson, for his untiring support and encouragement, and Paul Norcross, for his sharp insight and constructive comments. I also want to thank Jan Magiera who was instrumental in helping to finalize the manuscript.

There are many others to thank, too numerous to mention, who have helped with their prayers, love and financial support. Thank you from the bottom of my heart.

Table of Contents

Acknowledgements i
Table of Contents iii
Introduction 1
Chapter 1 A Rude Awakening 5
Chapter 2 The Journey to Blessing................21
Chapter 3 The Source of Blessing.................33
Chapter 4 Overflowing Blessings..................45
Chapter 5 Does God Curse?...........................73
Chapter 6 Innocent Blood............................97
Chapter 7 Known By Our Fruit...................113
Chapter 8 Cursed by Disobedience..............123
Chapter 9 What Is In Your Home?...............135
Chapter 10 Self-imposed Curses..................149
Chapter 11 The Curse of Poverty.................159
Chapter 12 Jesus Was Made a Curse For Us...163
Chapter 13 A New Beginning......................177
Appendix 1 183
About the Author......................................189
Order Form..191

Introduction

The subject of curses and blessings is often unfamiliar to students of the Bible. Yet God has much to say about them. Surprisingly, despite the clear fact that Jesus hung on the tree, and became a curse for every man to redeem us from the curse of the law (Galatians 3:13), we nevertheless must still deal with curses. How can I say such a thing if Christ finished our involvement with curses? Revelation 22, the closing chapter of the entire Bible speaks to this very question.

Revelation 22:3
And there shall be no more curse: but the throne of God and of the Lamb shall be in it; and his servants shall serve him:

The fact is that curses are still with us. What Jesus Christ accomplished on the cross was this: He gave every child of God the freedom to get out from under curses. This was one of His final acts by hanging on a tree. But clearly from Revelation 22:3, curses still exist and must be dealt with in the practical Christian walk.

The same argument is true regarding healing. Though by His stripes we were healed (I Peter 2:24), are all Christians healed today? No. But can they be if they reach out in faith to receive what Jesus accomplished for us on the cross? Yes. So it is with curses.

The problem with dealing with curses is that up until now, they have been generally obscure and hidden from Christian thought. While various religions around the world have become professionals at using curses (such as witchcraft, voodoo, tribal witchdoctors and medicine men, etc.) against the people of God, Christians themselves are largely ignorant of how to deal with curses. All this despite the fact that Jesus clearly enabled us to do so!

The very opposite of a curse is a blessing. Not only can Christians, by the accomplishments of Jesus Christ, learn to claim their liberty from curses, but they can also learn to receive blessings in place of those curses.

In *Turning Curses Into Blessings*, Carl Fox shows how the Lord led Him to expose this gap in the Body of Christ. I know of no other minister in Christian circles today whose ministry is accompanied by such extraordinary miracles---even the big names of the day. Having ministered with him personally across both the United States as well as overseas, I continue to marvel at how God uses this simple, humble man to bring deliverance to God's people where many others have failed.

It is not that one individual is particularly anointed over another, for we see too much such attention in the Body of Christ. But it is simply that the Lord has taught Carl this important field of turning the curses that plague God's people into blessings, so he in turn could teach to the rest of the people of God.

May the Lord continue to open the eyes of our understanding as we pursue our relationship with Him. And may your heart be as thrilled as mine has been to see how the Lord will turn our curses into blessings as we learn to obey Him.

Paul Norcross
Kingdom Faith Ministries
Charlemont, Massachusetts

Chapter 1
A Rude Awakening

"Do you remember this man?" asked a group of ministers who came up to me after a gathering in a university hall a few years ago. They pointed to a man in the group who kept grinning from ear to ear and waving at me. But I had no recollection of seeing him before.

It was a chilly fall night and I was in western Ukraine with a fellow minister who was teaching an accredited Bible College course. In those days in western Ukraine, nobody smiled and waved—they were still under great oppression, even though the Iron Curtain had already been lifted. What was there to be happy about in a place so devastated that many people died every winter from the cold and hunger? The government-run heating plants were broken down and the Communist governments that had held this nation in bondage since 1922 had taken all the spare parts when they departed in the 1980's. The very young, the very old, and the unhealthy perished every winter.

A smiling, happy man just didn't look normal for that environment. The men who had asked me to identify the happy fellow went on to tell me that he was the one they had brought to me for prayer the night before.

Not many people go to the western part of the Ukraine. It is very difficult to get into this part of the country, and there is no guarantee that you can get out once you are in. This area used to have a secret city where Russian spies were trained during the Cold War before coming to the West. The interpreters that were hired, avowed atheists and communists, had formerly taught English to the spies that came to the West. The Christian minister in charge of the translation work during the class had to monitor their work closely. But while helping with the translating, they accepted Jesus as their Lord and they started showing the fruit of the Spirit that had changed their hearts and lives.

The Russian Mafia has so much control there now that it is a bad situation and Christians are still suffering very much. This area is so different from most of Eastern Europe, because the Ukraine fell under Communism in 1922, not in the 40's, like the rest of Eastern Europe. Right after World War I, Russia overpowered them and then they lost their identity.

Immediately after Russia took over, the Ukrainian language was made illegal and so was Jesus Christ. Anyone who used the name of Jesus was killed. The churches were required to support propaganda programs during the daytime, so people could hold church services only after 8 p.m. No young people were allowed and the name of Jesus and the Ukrainian language were forbidden.

Every church, even the Orthodox, had nicely-kept graves in the back for the martyrs who had refused to

A RUDE AWAKENING

stop naming the name of Jesus. In our nation, the United States, we are very fortunate. People in this nation commonly use His name in vain or slanderously, but in the western Ukraine, most people have never even heard the name of Jesus, even as a swear word. So where do you start in a place like this to reach people with the name of Jesus and the love of God? We just had to trust the Lord to give us the way to do it.

At the hall, where we held evening meetings for the general public to tell them about Jesus and God, I stood in the back and offered to pray for healing and deliverance for anyone who was sick—something these Ukrainians had never heard of. The very first night we did this, things were slow, but once people started getting healed and delivered, they started bringing others to be prayed for. Even though they had never heard of Jesus, given the seventy years of their captivity in atheism, they knew about spiritual power with long experience with witchcraft. Witchcraft was the leading spiritual power over there. The man who was brought to me the night before had been cursed with a professional curse by witches. I guess that he figured in order to get rid of the curse he had to go to a clairvoyant, which compounded his problems!

The whole village knew that the man, whom I will call Slava, was cursed. They were familiar with that kind of spiritual power. No one would do business with him, leaving him without income. His mother-in-law had come down with a virus and was dying of dehydration. His mother had a stroke and was paralyzed. The whole family with all the children was living in a one-bedroom house with no food or money. And to top it all off, the roof had caved in on part of their house. When someone brought Slava to me for prayer, without thinking twice about it, I removed the curses from him in the name of Jesus, because I was confident that that was what God said to do. Then I went on to pray for the next person and many others, totally forgetting about the cursed man.

The next night when he showed up at the meeting, the people explained through our interpreter what had happened. I had prayed to remove the curses. He had gone home to find that his mother-in-law—who had been dehydrated, dying with a virus, and who hadn't been able to eat—was up making cabbage soup! She was feeling great and was just hungry. They went to bed very late that night because there was great rejoicing in their house. When they got up the next morning, his mother, who had been paralyzed for months, was sitting on the edge of the bed working on getting her balance.

There was no real reason to hurry down to the shop, because nobody was doing business with him anymore. They hadn't had this much rejoicing in a long while. It was about two o'clock in the afternoon when he finally got down to the shop. When he arrived, people were lined up all the way down the street waiting for him to come. The strange thing was

A RUDE AWAKENING

that nobody knew that things had changed in his house. Yet, there had been an about-face regarding everything in their lives.

When they told me about what had happened to this man, I thought to myself, "I've got to learn about this," but we were so busy that I did not think that much about it again. That was a big mistake! I had no idea I would suffer consequences as a result of my lack of knowledge of how powerful curses really are. I was new to the whole idea and God was using this incident with the man to teach me. It turned out to be a very hard lesson, because without really thinking it out, I had stirred up the devils in the witches who had cursed the man.

You see, just being oblivious to something does not mean it can't happen. You may say, "Oh, well, it won't hurt me to step off this building." But when you hit the ground, it's still going to hurt you, even if you don't know what gravity is—if you happen to live through it.

The consequences began while we were still in the Ukraine. We had an incident with the Ukrainian army, "the big guns," and had a hard time getting out of the country. At the time, it never even occurred to us that anything serious was happening, much less that we had been cursed. I was caught in a no-man zone between the borders of Hungary and the Ukraine for hours. These countries usually have no-man zones about a block wide. It was a bitterly cold day, with no place to take shelter, and I was wearing very little

TURNING CURSES TO BLESSINGS

clothing. We had given most of our clothes away before returning home. The weather had been warmer when we arrived in the Ukraine, but it had turned very cold by the time we returned to Budapest.

When we got back to the eastern United States, even stranger things were happening. I hadn't slept for four days; I just couldn't sleep. My wife was waiting for me in the Southeast and we still needed to drive across the country to our home in New Mexico. So I said, "We might as well go back home now, because I can't sleep." We took off. We were on the Interstate Highway 20 and it was raining so hard we couldn't see, when **both** my back tires went flat. There was nothing we could do about it—we couldn't get anyone to stop to help us. Finally, after sitting there for about three hours, still not able to sleep, I just started driving and prayed, "God, please protect our tire rims." So, we drove thumpety-thump, two or three miles an hour for miles, until we reached the next exit. When we got there we found a mechanic's garage, but the people wouldn't help us. This really happened! I was getting very puzzled and questioning why this was all happening.

It was the middle of the night and we didn't know if we should go on from that gas station. Then I remembered we had an Auto Club card, so I called them, and they came to help. They towed us about twenty miles to a tire dealership, where they dropped us in front of the garage doors. There we sat for a couple of hours until the workers showed up and

A RUDE AWAKENING

even **they** were unfriendly! After we bought a couple of new tires, we got all the way home safely.

Finally, on arriving home in Albuquerque, I found out that my business had been totally dead for many days. Everything had just come to a complete stop. Everything! I found out that people, who had loved us before, now were being spiteful. The people who were going to help us financially with the trip did not come through with the money promised, so we were extremely deep in debt. I fasted and prayed until I received a word from the Lord. It consisted of one word only, "curse," that's all. I picked up the phone to call a friend and he asked me, "Were you messing around with witches in Russia?" I said, "No, I was not messing around with witches! And I was in Ukraine, not Russia!" Then I remembered the incident with the man who was cursed.

We went out to pray at the sand dunes near Albuquerque. The view there is amazing. From those hills of sand on the high desert, I could see mountain ranges all around us, some as much as a hundred miles away. As I prayed, I'd watch storms come and go and move around. In this awesome beauty, I would sense God's presence very strongly. This was one of my favorite praying places, with the sand blowing like drifting snow. For two or three hours, we praised God and prayed. When we got back, the phone was ringing—boom! Business was flowing again. Out on the dunes I had prayed in the name of the Lord Jesus Christ, asking God to remove all the curses I had

TURNING CURSES TO BLESSINGS

picked up, and thanking Him for blessing us even though we were hurting and our business had been shut down on us. The curses were broken, business was back to normal, and we continued to ask God for everything to work well. We started receiving blessings again instead of being cursed.

That incident started me on a quest with God to understand about curses and how they can be broken. Little did I know at the time that I would end up traveling all over the world teaching about this subject. I have taught the topic as a class called *"Turning Curses to Blessings"* over two hundred times and have traveled to three different continents. By God's grace, thousands of people have been healed of diseases and bad health conditions. Many have been delivered from oppression. Blind people can now see and deaf people can now hear. People have been healed of back problems, heart problems, emotional problems, and economic problems. People have had marriage problems from generational curses. God showed them to us and we removed them in the name of Jesus. Then later those same people would tell us things like, "You're right! I'm from a third generation of divorcees!" All of these miracles have happened as a result of finding the curses and replacing them with blessings from God.

Let me make something very clear. All this has happened to us, not because I'm such a great person, but because I have been willing to do whatever God asks me to do. I'm just an ordinary man (and not too

A RUDE AWAKENING

good a one, at that), but God is extraordinary and awesome! The visions He has given me and the things He has taught me have tremendously enriched my own life. I have had to put up with a lot of issues in my life and now I know how to deal with them.

Now I understand how they can be solved and the authority that Satan had over me before has been broken. I want to emphasize again that this has nothing to do with my being a special person. All the glory goes to God for any time anyone is healed or delivered. The promise of God is: **"And whatsoever ye shall ask in my name, that will I do, that the Father may be glorified in the Son. If ye shall ask any thing in my name, I will do it. If ye love me, keep my commandments" (John 14:13-15).**

Let me tell you a little about my background. As a small child, I used to speak to and hear from God, singing, and talking to Him as I ran down the deer trails in northern Minnesota. My communication with God was good, until there were a series of incidents in the church that caused me to rebel against God. You see, I believed that the church represented God. As time elapsed, I drew closer to the Lord and I began to ask convicting questions—the kind that make some ministers nervous when persistent little kids ask honest questions. There soon came a time when I was rejected by the church. When they rejected me, I felt God had rejected me and I blamed God. It was then that I decided I was not going to have anything more

TURNING CURSES TO BLESSINGS

to do with the things of God. I became intensely angry and rebellious. A lot of deep-rooted curses had come through our bloodline—all the way from Ireland! A curse of anger and other curses really affected us after my whole family left the church.

Prior to that time, I had a good relationship with my family members, but something happened that caused us to be driven away from each other. After that, family relationships deteriorated. Around that time, my uncle and my father got into a violent fight. No one ever saw my uncle again—ever! My brother and I didn't have anything to do with each other for twenty-five years. Years later, once I understood how curses worked against our family, I talked to my brother and we prayed. We became the best of friends after all those years! These curses are real! And they happen all over the world, not just to the Irish!

After I stopped going to church, I no longer looked to God for answers. Life became very difficult for me. I was a rebellious teenager working as a hand on my father's farm. I left home at seventeen to make my own way in life. I worked at all kinds of jobs until I finally started working as a life insurance salesman. I became very successful in business and I built up my own insurance agency. I was earning a high income from it, as well as from several other businesses I started. I had the world at my feet or so I thought!

Ever since being rejected from the church, there was always a thread of anger, hatred, and violence that colored all my actions. I never had peace in my heart.

A RUDE AWAKENING

I was always on the offensive and experienced a lot of rejection in personal relationships. My anger curse didn't help too much, either. Barroom brawls, fights, angry reactions, and revenges were a common occurrence. I was smart enough to keep good working relationships for the sake of business, but was forever restless, always looking for the next challenge, never satisfied.

It was not until I was about thirty years old that I finally made my peace with God again. At that point, I resolved to serve Him and do what He told me, in spite of the cost. This was a new beginning in my life, a time of new challenges and new things happening to me. I couldn't even begin to tell you of all the times that God protected me, times when I was sure there were angels looking after me. I lived in many places, met many people, and talked to them about the mercy of God for them. I also met my lovely wife, Sheila. We were living in Albuquerque, New Mexico, when I finally began to understand for the first time about all those unexplainable things in my life and in the lives of others.

EXPLAINING THE UNEXPLAINABLE

There are so many questions we ask ourselves. Why are the Irish always fighting each other? Why are there so many poor people in certain countries? Do the gypsies **always** have to roam around? Why can't the Israelis and the Arabs get along, when they are

TURNING CURSES TO BLESSINGS

both descendents of Father Abraham? How come some people get sick and the doctors are never able to do anything to heal them? What does it mean when certain countries in the world just can't seem to stop having revolutions and live in peace?

I've discovered that when we ask God these questions, He will always answer them so we can learn to live a life full of rich blessings, instead of one that is cursed and tormented. We have many questions in our own personal lives that seem totally unanswerable and people conveniently say to us, "You'll just have to wait until you go to heaven so that God can tell you."

I'll tell you, I have asked Him many questions! Now I'll ask you. Did you know that God curses people? Do you know that many times you curse yourself and don't even know it? How about all the people who curse you and don't even realize they are doing something so bad? Do you know about professional curses? Have you ever seen a man of God curse someone, in the name of God? Curses are powerful things and nobody wants them in their life.

I have seen how curses operate in different cultures with different people. Certain races of people have things in their culture or history that cause curses. One day, here in America, an Apache Indian from New Mexico came over to my house. He was drunk and upset because of what white men did to the Indians, including introducing them to alcohol. So I said to him, "I wonder who laid out the biggest curse, us or you?"

A RUDE AWAKENING

And he asked, "What do you mean?"

I said, "Well, the white man didn't know anything about smoking tobacco, either—until they connected with the Indians. I wonder which caused the greatest problem: alcohol or tobacco?"

He got really mad at me and said that was not true. So I asked him, "Are you calling me a liar in my own home?"

He replied, "No, but it just is not true."

I responded, "Well, you're drunk and you're not very polite, so hit the road. Get out of here!" He was belligerent.

A week later, he came back and he said, "Preacher, I have to tell you, I'm sorry."

I said, "For what?"

Then he answered, "Because you told the truth and I called you a liar."

The interesting thing about this incident is that we became friends. I discovered he was a medicine man. Over a period of time, I talked to him about Jesus Christ. He confessed Jesus as Lord and renounced all his practices of witchcraft. At this time, he was born again into the family of God, delivered from the power of evil, and healed in his body. He even brought several friends to me so they could get the "whole works" too!

But, when he fell back into alcohol, he came back to our place drunken and belligerent. I told him he had to leave until he sobered up. The next day we found feathers stuck all over our property in the

TURNING CURSES TO BLESSINGS

manner of Indian witchcraft. He had laid curses on us, because he didn't know anything else. That was just his way of doing things.

Have you ever wondered why American Indians have historically had a much lower tolerance for alcohol than white settlers? Many become alcoholics and don't have to drink very much to get drunk. I believe the curse is in their blood—I say this with all respect, because I have dear friends who are American Indians.

There are also certain things that are unique about the Russians and the Germans, as well as other Caucasian groups. Here in the United States people tend to classify all white people together, but they are really distinct white races. These races come from different parts of Europe and you often encounter different curses on them. Some people wouldn't want to call them that, but it's true!

When I look at the curses that came on this land because of slavery, I see that they caused a war that we still have not recovered from in some areas of the country. I believe the bitterness is still there. Also, many blacks have not truly received freedom. The situation, in which blacks in Africa sold their brothers and sisters into slavery, and the subsequent enslavement in this country, brought many curses on them, both in Africa and America. We see this in the gangs on the streets of America today.

But what about the good things in life? Do you ever wish **something** would go right for you? How

A RUDE AWAKENING

many times have you desired to have good relationships with people and something keeps messing you up? Have you ever read books about when bad things happen to good people? How would you like to read a book about how good things could happen to bad people?" God wants to turn the bad into good in my life and He wants to do it in yours.

My story is only an example to help you, the reader, understand that I am just like you—probably worse—and God has used me, and is using me, to help people come out of conditions that are out of control in their lives. There's no way I could have been good enough to deserve His favor. If there is anything in this book that speaks to you, to your situation, and helps you to get free, all the honor and respect and glory belong to God and Jesus Christ. Jesus Christ is the only way to be rescued from man's sinful condition! He is our freedom and our peace. Look for Him and you will find Him; ask Him and you'll receive; open yourself up to Him and He will communicate with you and you with Him. God says that if you don't ask, you don't receive. So, what's wrong with asking? Nothing! It's great, because He does answer!

This book is all about turning bad to good and many things more! So, put on your seat belt and take a ride with me. I pray you'll never be the same after this trip and you will walk in God's blessings all the days of your life!

Chapter 2
The Journey to Blessing

I was out elk hunting on a nice, warm, sunny day. My gun was probably ten feet away from me, lying on the ground, because I was not paying attention to the elk. I was just having a good time talking with the Lord! I was enjoying the sunshine on that nice fall day in the rugged mountains of the Gila Wilderness near the Arizona-New Mexico border. Untouched by human hands, God had made the beauty that surrounded me. I could feel His presence there. At that point, in my ministry I was seeing great results when I broke curses, but I didn't really understand a lot of things. I started talking with God about the issue of curses, where they come from, and what they are.

"Well," He said, "a curse that's causeless cannot land. However, if you're in disobedience, that's when you're open to being cursed." He stated that basically to stay away from being cursed you have to always obey. He asked me if I had ever met a Christian who always obeyed. "No, I have not," I said, "especially me!"

He pointed out to me some buzzards that were circling. They had been circling for about an hour out over the canyon in front of me, in the air currents. Then He said, "That's the way curses are. They'll hang around for a long time waiting for a chance to come in." He said, "Eventually they've got to go back to where they came from, if they can't come in."

TURNING CURSES TO BLESSINGS

Later, I found this verse in Proverbs that states this principle:

(Proverbs 26:2) As the bird by wandering, as the swallow by flying, so the curse causeless shall not come.

A few days later, I had a vision. In this vision, I saw a big wall between mankind and evil. As I looked, I could see evil spirits constantly coming and going through the wall. When I looked closer, I saw that the doors all had locks on them. I knew that those locks were God's protection. So, how did the spirits keep coming and going? I looked even closer and saw that the evil spirits each had a key that let them through!

So I asked God, "Why do these evil spirits have keys?" He answered, "The keys are curses that give the spirits legal authority to come in. There are many kinds of keys: some are inherited—or generational—curses, some are self-imposed, others have to do with behavior, when people disobey the words I have given them."

If you don't want the evil spirits to have authority in your life, you have to make sure any curses on you have been broken. A curse can't land on you unless it has a cause. Fear and sin are basically the two main causes, which take the blessings out of your life. Sin definitely does that! When God says in the Bible to do something and you say, "Well, I don't feel like doing it, I'm not going to do it," you have left yourself open to sin which results in getting cursed. God will not let Satan cause us harm unless we leave a legal opening. The devil is a "legal beagle" (a legalistic being) and if you leave a legal opening for him to hit you, he will surely use it. It would be illegal to curse you without a cause. God would smash his head right in and the day will come for that!

People can't understand why curses land and why they get them. Our society has come to the point where we have made sin so acceptable that we say, "I'm sorry," on the run and do not really repent. Repentance means to turn away and change our actions. True repentance and confession of sin will allow God to protect us completely.

One other important point is that we're not to be so curse-centered that we don't see the blessings of God. We're not to be curse crusaders! That's not what God wants. He does not want us to be so curse-conscious that we don't enjoy our fellowship with Him and don't permit Him to have closeness with us.

But we have to realize that if we leave an opening for curses to come in, they are going to come in. We need to say, "Hey, I don't want the curses. I want to be rid of them." That's why 1 John 1:9 is so very important, because **"if we confess our sins, He is faithful and just to forgive us our sins, and to cleanse us from all unrighteousness."** Disobedience is a sin, so, by confession, you take away the key and the devil has no authority in that area of your life.

TURNING CURSES TO BLESSINGS

A CURSE MUST BE REPLACED WITH A BLESSING

When I returned from working in the Ukraine, my back was literally up against the wall. I didn't know where to go, but as I pursued an understanding of the subject of curses and how to get rid of them, the Lord started turning things around very quickly. In place of the curses, blessings from the Lord began to flow to us. Many people encouraged me to teach what I was learning out of the Word of God. So I said, "OK," and thought I would teach it once.

From the very beginning, I realized that this subject of turning curses into blessings was going to be hard to teach because there is so much in the Bible about it. So, instead of just waiting around until I had exhausted all research on the subject, I put myself on the spot by setting a date. Then I really did have to be ready!

I remember the day before I was going to teach, I was up on the mountain with a friend praying and asking the Lord for His help. A voice behind us said, "Whenever you remove a curse, be sure to replace it with a blessing." We both turned around at the same time and there was nobody there. We had no doubt who had spoken. We both heard the voice!

I needed to document this in the Word of God before I could teach it, and I didn't have time to search scripture to prove it, but God is so gracious! A friend called me that night and said, "Carl, since you've been studying this stuff about curses, you need to look at this scripture. It says that God will turn your curses into blessings." Here is the verse that sets the foundation for the class and is the cornerstone of this book:

(Deuteronomy 23:5) "But the LORD thy God turned the curse into a blessing unto thee, because the LORD thy God loved thee."

This is where we hit a milestone on the journey in understanding. This is the biggest and probably the most misunderstood principle that God has taught us about this subject. Not only do we need to get rid of the curses, but also **we need to put blessings in their place.** The best thing about it all is that the blessings work much stronger and last much longer than do the curses!

Too many people get offended when I mention that a lot of their problems could be the result of curses. They'll say, "Oh, I don't have anything to do with curses! That's witchcraft and sorcery and I never touch that stuff. Besides, I don't have any enemies that would want to curse me." But the strangest thing is that when people who are Christians get mad at me, they quote the verse:

TURNING CURSES TO BLESSINGS

(Galatians 3:13) Christ hath redeemed us from the curse of the law, being made a curse for us.

They say that no curses could have any power because we are born again. Don't they read the Bible? Jesus paid the price on the cross for our complete redemption, which includes being free from curses, but just as with everything else He made available, we have to claim it in our lives.

If you're sick, what's the first thing you do? You start finding out everything you can about what's happening in your body—whether you go to a doctor, a specialist, read about it in books and magazines or talk to people who have the same symptoms. Some people even go on the Internet to find out what's wrong. If you think you have measles, or pneumonia or cancer, and a doctor confirms it, even if you don't like that sickness, you're happy to have a diagnosis that will get you going in some direction for treatment and, hopefully, for a cure.

If bad things were happening to you, wouldn't you want to know why—even if it was a curse like the one put on the Ukrainian fellow I mentioned in Chapter One? He knew he was cursed, because he was from a place where that sort of thing was openly known and talked about. His problem was that he got cursed twice by trying to get someone to go against whoever cursed him. He should have gone to God first, but he was glad to hear there was a solution to

THE JOURNEY TO BLESSING

his problems—that God cared enough for him to offer him one. That's why it is so important to understand what a curse is. That was the next thing that God unfolded to me in my studies in the Scripture.

WHAT IS A CURSE?

A curse starts with an utterance. It is something that is said out of the mouth, whether a prayer, a word, an oath, an expression, or a pronouncement. The following are some dictionary definitions of a curse:

<u>Britannica World Encyclopedia</u>: An imprecation of evil, any profane oath; calamity invoked or threatened.

<u>Webster's Dictionary</u>: A prayer that harm or injury may come upon someone; a word or an expression used in cursing or swearing;

<u>American Heritage Dictionary</u>: An appeal to a supernatural power for evil or injury to befall someone or something. To invoke evil, calamity or injury upon; to damn.

Wherever we see a lack of blessings, there is definitely a curse. A curse is intended to do evil to someone. It starts with an utterance—just as a

TURNING CURSES TO BLESSINGS

blessing does. Blessings and curses both start with utterances, and the words are very powerful. God framed the world with words. When He wanted light, He didn't build a power company, He spoke words, "Let there be light!" That light included all that we experience here on earth: color, life, and energy. Words have great authority. Negative words give Satan the authority to operate against us to steal, kill, and destroy, as in the case of Job. God acts upon our positive words to bring us a blessed life. That's why we have to be really careful about what we say. When they are in trouble, many people make their problems worse by saying, "Oh, Lord! I'm suffering! I can't take much more!" They are actually dumping curses on themselves (self-imposed curses) because of what they are saying. God's instruction is to pray His answer to the problem and to confess the promises of His Word.

Whether a curse is intentional, put on you by someone else or by yourself, it always starts with words. Satan himself can't curse you—he can only use words spoken out to bring on a curse. If a person says he can't do something and keeps saying it, he never gets it done. If children are told that they are stupid many times and that is repeated to them over and over, they spend their whole life being stupid, even though they are actually very intelligent. Telling someone they are stupid is a curse because of the power of the words spoken against them. The power of the utterance is something that will go on and on throughout that person's life. Those evil words entrench themselves into his or her mind and get even more embedded into their personality, unless something is done about it.

We will see in the next few chapters what God says about curses. But right now, let us look at the definition of what is a blessing. It is much more important to know the blessings He has for us if we believe Him and are obedient. He says in Jeremiah 29:11 that **"For I know the thoughts that I think toward you, saith the Lord, thoughts of peace, and not of evil, to give you an expected end."** Too many times, it looks like bad things happen to us totally unexpectedly, but God wants to show us how to expect blessings. He is awesome! He wants to pour out His blessings to us in every category.

WHAT IS A BLESSING?

A blessing also starts with an utterance. It is to speak well of or to praise God. You can bless God by your life, by loving Him and obeying Him. When we praise God, we are blessing Him; we speak blessings to God and to Jesus! Here are some dictionary definitions of a blessing:

Britannica World Encyclopedia: That which makes happy or prosperous; a gift of divine favor; a benediction; grateful adoration; worship.

TURNING CURSES TO BLESSINGS

<u>Webster's Dictionary</u>: The act of one that blesses; approval; a thing conducive to happiness or welfare; grace said at a meal.

<u>American Heritage Dictionary</u>: An expression or utterance of good wishes; anything promoting or contributing to happiness, well-being or prosperity.

God also has blessings toward man. Some of His blessings are His goodness and promises and favor and mercy. We all need God's blessings. God's mercy is a blessing. Eternal life is a blessing that we have no idea how to comprehend. About a million years from now, we're going to scratch our heads and say, "You know, this is a good deal!"

Because blessings start with words, when we speak the blessings of God to a person in the name of Jesus Christ, those things are imparted into their lives. When we speak blessings into a person's life, these blessings have much more authority and power than do curses. When we tell our children, "You are a blessing," "You are wonderful," and "God brought you as a blessing to our family," we are setting them up for happiness and prosperity in their adult lives. So many times kids are told that they were brought into the world as an accident and other things like that. There are even parents who tell their children, "I don't love you," or "You'll never amount to much,"

THE JOURNEY TO BLESSING

which causes them to spend their whole life living under the curse of those words.

Putting blessings into the marriage of a young couple is a very common thing. I won't officiate at a wedding unless I get a chance to get rid of the curses first, so love can have authority in that marriage. That's one of my requirements. Whenever I perform a wedding, I must be allowed to get rid of the curses. Just because two people love each other so much that they can't keep their hands off each other, can't say good night or think about anything else besides the handsome dude or the doll they are in love with, does not mean their marriage will go well.

As soon as they get married, the devil enforces the "one flesh" principle, which God says that when we marry we become one. The devil attacks the marriage right away and before very long, the lovers can't stand each other. How? Why can he do that? Because they have each lived with their own curses all their lives. Each one was used to his or her own curses; but now they have their partner's curses too. Because they are one flesh, the curses get exchanged between them. If these things are broken and the couple is liberated from their own curses without picking up each other's curses, then you can talk about this union coming together and being powerful. A marriage that starts with the blessings of God can be a great example and blessing to the Body of Christ.

Chapter 3
The Source of Blessing

All blessing originally comes from God. Have you ever heard the devil bless you? Can you imagine Satan wanting anything good for you? If he ever says anything like that, you can be sure it's a lie. He's trying to trick you into thinking he has your best interests in mind, so that you'll fall into his trap. God is the source of all blessing and when He blesses, you're enriched and you get no sorrow with it! Happiness, health, and prosperity are things that God wants for all of us:

(3 John 2) Beloved, I wish above all things that thou mayest prosper and be in health, even as thy soul prospereth.

There's a great account in the Bible, which talks about a man who lived about four thousand years ago over where Iraq is now. This man really knew God. And because of him, you and I have received some great blessings from God.

(Genesis 12:1-4) Now the LORD had said unto Abram, Get thee out of thy country, and from thy kindred, and from thy father's house, unto a land that I will show thee:
And I will make of thee a great nation, and I will bless thee, and make thy name great; and thou shalt be a blessing;

TURNING CURSES TO BLESSINGS

And I will bless them that bless thee, and curse him that curseth thee: and in thee shall all families of the earth be blessed.

So Abram departed, as the LORD had spoken unto him; and Lot went with him: and Abram was seventy and five years old when he departed out of Haran.

Did you see that? All families of the earth shall be blessed! That's us! We're all descendents of Abraham, if we have faith. He is our father of faith. Abraham is our father and because of this, God will bless us. This is a profound statement and a true one. **"I will bless those who bless you, and curse those that curse you."** Abraham set the standard, because he obeyed the word of the Lord. This is something we can all have, if we obey. **Obedience is the key!** When we obey, we get blessed.

We are descendants of Abraham by faith and it is very important that we realize we do not have to fight against people. I tell those who want to be antagonistic towards me, "If you bless me, you're blessed, and I'll love you even if you curse me—but you're still going to be cursed. Do you know why? Because Abraham is my father of faith. I have inherited this blessing."

We don't always have to be busy getting even anymore. It makes quite a difference! We don't have to fight the battle. Before I turned to the Lord, I used to be the kind of man who would go out and get

THE SOURCE OF BLESSING

even. I was really into "Vengeance is mine, says Carl!" It wouldn't bother me a bit to throw a man out of the car at 70 miles an hour on the freeway. That's the kind of man I used to be! But now I really believe that **"Vengeance is mine; I will repay, saith the Lord" (Romans 12:19).** And now I pray that God's vengeance will be that the person repents and comes into the family of God. It's my business to love. It's not my business to hate.

For example, one time I prayed for a lady who had a brain tumor and was due for surgery two days later to take it out. When God healed her of the tumor and she told the people of her religious denomination about it, they said to her, "That man heals with the power of the devil!" I was so mad that I went out into the wilderness and started screaming out to the Lord about it. Guess what Jesus said to me? He said: "You should have heard all the things the religious leaders said to me and about me!" So, what was I going to do? I needed to repent and ask the Lord to forgive me. Then I could pray for those people.

It is great how God has things set up. You don't need to go to the Ouija board or crystal ball to figure these things out. It's here in black and white in the Bible! You have, through our father of faith, Abraham, the ability to be blessed—to know that if you bless someone and if you obey, you're blessed. And when people bless you, they are blessed. These are principles God established from olden times, and they are still relevant to us in the age of grace today.

Was Abraham disobedient when God told him to get out? Did he say, "I don't feel like leaving. All my relatives are here. I'm staying here. Get lost, God?" No, he didn't. He left Haran as the Lord spoke to him. Abraham was seventy-five years old when he left his home and family. This is a straightforward example of God blessing those who are obedient to His instruction. Even if His command does not make sense to you, when you obey it, you are blessed. How about letting Him prove His word to you? How about being simple about obeying as He instructs? Sometimes people with all the religious theology and doctrines don't have a clue about how to obey. The first sin in the Garden of Eden was about knowledge. It included the knowledge of **good**, not just of evil.

BLESSINGS COME FROM GOD BY OBEDIENCE

God loves to bless us when we don't hold back anything from Him that He has asked us for. Abraham not only obeyed God down to the letter, but he didn't hold back his son for whom he had waited for so long. He was a hundred years old and his wife was ninety and they hadn't been able to have any children. So, when they finally had the promised son that God had spoken of, God turned around and asked him for his son back—sacrificed on an altar! I

THE SOURCE OF BLESSING

don't know if I could have done that. You probably already know the story, but just as he's ready to kill his son on a pile of rocks, and angel of the Lord calls out of heaven and stops him.

Abraham changed all of our lives—he was an example of God and his son was an example of Jesus.

(Genesis 22:15-18) And the angel of the LORD called unto Abraham out of heaven the second time,

And said, By myself have I sworn, saith the LORD, for because thou hast done this thing, and hast not withheld thy son, thine only son:

That in blessing I will bless thee, and in multiplying I will multiply thy seed as the stars of the heaven, and as the sand which is upon the sea shore; and thy seed shall possess the gate of his enemies;

There's nothing here about going to war, is there? Is not that amazing? It says we shall possess the gates of our enemies. Do you know how this happens? By obedience, just like Abraham.

Obedience is a very important key to avoid curses. If God says to do something, who do we think we are to sit back and wait for Him to talk us into it? How many times do we just put something off? Abraham didn't do that. Isaac was no twelve or thirteen year-old child at this time. I believe that he was about thirty years old. That would have made his Papa one hundred thirty years old. He could have said, "Hey, old man, you've had your life—let's barbecue **you**!" Isaac knew the power of obedience, just like his father did. He knew that if he obeyed God he would be all right, because he knew that God did not lie when He made promises. If he died on that altar, if he died in that fire and sacrifice, there would be no promise. That is how we obey God. If He said it, He really means it, even if it looks impossible! They traveled for three days and Abraham didn't carry anything with him to sacrifice.

I'll bet Abraham had some doubt to deal with! And don't you think that about an hour into the journey, Isaac was starting to wonder, after he had been taking inventory on what was loaded up into the four-wheeler? "Just a second, Dad! We don't have any lamb here!" If we will believe God, we can overcome doubt. We don't have to figure out how He's going to do it! We don't have to! If we start trying to figure out how God is going to do something, that's exactly how we **don't** get it done! We can set aside the doubt and do what God asks. The results will follow.

I get called into situations in which I have no idea what's going to happen. I just try to be obedient to the Lord. I remember there was one time with a poor girl who had been seeking deliverance for ten years. She had so many devils in her life, and her daddy was a pastor. It was a tragedy in that family. When she started to get rid of the devils, what happened was

THE SOURCE OF BLESSING

amazing. There were people standing around watching and praying, so I told them to start singing praises to the Lord. Satan does not like that and God does! Also, it attracts the angels and we needed some help. Then Satan said to me very clearly (he does not usually talk to me): "Look at these people, they think you really know what you're doing!" I just told him, "No, but I know who does!" That is the key. That girl got delivered and to this day, she's delivered. And the church changed because of what happened that day in the girl's life. It was not the praise that delivered the girl; it was obedience to the revelation of the Lord.

It is God's heart that all "should be saved and come to a knowledge of Him." That's a real blessing that God wants for mankind. We don't have to get into difficult theology about what is God's will in this matter. If the heavens are like brass, I know a quick way to get brass to melt—with heat and with praise! Just start praising God! Praise is always God's will.

I learned a lesson about praise one time. I went to pray for a man who had cancer. He was bedridden, in agony, a sack of bones. His wife was down the road in the office trying to keep the business afloat. So, not thinking, I went into his room and asked him, "Hey man, what've you been doing all day?" As soon as I asked the question, I realized it was very insensitive of me. But as I asked it, I looked into his eyes and saw a man with so much life in him. He answered, "What can a man in my position do? I've been praising God all day!" Now, that's the sacrifice of praise!

TURNING CURSES TO BLESSINGS

We obey God by continually praising Him. There are so many intercessors that spend so much time doing warfare and very little praising God. If they would praise God more, the warfare would go quickly. You'll draw so many angels around you. Angels "encamp around those who do warfare," right? No, that's not what it says; it says, **"The angel of the Lord encampeth round about them that fear him, and delivereth them" (Psalm 34:7).** Real warfare is fearing God, praising and respecting Him. He's the General, the Commander in Chief. God's love is more powerful than a nuclear bomb. God's love takes away envy and jealousy. His perfect love casts out all fear. This is the kind of blessing that God has called us all to impart in Jesus' name.

Obedience is warfare. If God tells you to do something impossible, you should do it, because you're going to experience a miracle. Obedience presupposes that we make every effort not to sin. Those who say they have not sinned make God a liar. Do you want to face God with that in the Judgment Day? This is Scripture written for those of us who are already born again:

(1 John 1:9) If we confess our sins, he is faithful and just to forgive us our sins, and to cleanse us from all unrighteousness.

THE SOURCE OF BLESSING

The blood of Jesus was not just there to get us born again. It's there to keep us in fellowship with God Almighty, the Creator of the heavens and the earth, to have that sonship relationship. He wants to be a Daddy to us. He wants us to be so honest that when we sin we just come up to Him and say, "Father, forgive me."

We have sins that are habitual but sometimes there are also curses there that make us keep doing them. We can ask God to give us the strength not to do that sin anymore. Religion often excuses sin by saying, "That's not really a sin! Come on, man, we're living in the 21st century!!" But God is not fooled. What are we going to do with what God says, **"I am the Lord and I change not?"**

We have a responsibility for our lives, and that's how we're going to be blessed, if we learn to walk in the Spirit (which means to love), to stay dependent on the Lord Jesus Christ. To me, "Lord" means "Boss." In Romania, they say "Chef," which means boss. Jesus is a good boss; He's got a good health insurance package (3 John 2). You don't have to worry about social security. He gives you eternal life and He's not going to stick you into some rickety rest home. He's up there preparing mansions. By the way, He's not a Jewish carpenter. He's a church builder and a mansion builder. He said, "I'm going to prepare a place for you." We have a lot of reasons to serve God, a lot of reasons to let Him have lordship over our lives.

TURNING CURSES TO BLESSINGS

Our real freedom of will is not doing as we please and slowly changing our minds. Real freedom of will is doing what the Bible says. We have been purchased by the blood of Jesus Christ. We belong to Him! We deserve to be his slaves. He loves us and He changes us by loving us. Christianity is not a hard, miserable thing to do. It's like ice-skating, once you get on the ice, after learning how to do it, then you don't get tired. You just move smoothly all over. That's what Christianity is supposed to be for us. We just move with the Lord and He gives us the strength. He'll give us the answers, too, even if we think we don't need answers.

Abraham was asked to sacrifice his son Isaac and he loved God so much that he was willing to obey. God will bless us when we obey His word.

(Genesis 22:18) And in thy seed shall all the nations of the earth be blessed; because thou hast obeyed my voice.

It just does not matter what your skin color is, because the flesh is dead. The nations of the earth are blessed because we are God's children by faith. We fit into this picture. God's blessings are so profound that when we obey His Word, especially when it is something we don't want to do, that's when the blessings are the biggest.

If we want blessings, we have to obey God's voice. If He says don't do something, we must not do

THE SOURCE OF BLESSING

it! If we can't quit, an addiction, for example, we tell Him, and He'll give us the strength to quit. We cannot have God's blessings if we are out there doing as we please. We will be cursed at every turn. Not only that, Deuteronomy proves it will bring curses on our generations to come. The Bible says that the curses go on to your children forever.

(Deuteronomy 28:45, 46) Moreover all these curses shall come upon thee, and shall pursue thee, and overtake thee, till thou be destroyed; because thou hearkenedst not unto the voice of the Lord thy God, to keep his commandments and his statutes which he commanded thee:
And they shall be upon thee for a sign and for a wonder, and upon thy seed for ever.

In contrast, God is the source of all blessing and as we are obedient to His word, all the blessings shall overtake us.

(Deuteronomy 28:2) And all these blessings shall come on thee, and overtake thee, if thou shalt hearken unto the voice of the Lord thy God.

Chapter 4
Overflowing Blessings

The gypsy mother and her daughter smiled from ear to ear as they hurried out, wiping the tears from their eyes. Momma was healed! Her daughter, who was in her thirties, had all she could do to keep from laughing out of sheer joy! The heaviness was gone. Something had happened to her body, too. They could hardly wait to get home to tell the family what was going on. Their steps got lighter and lighter as they walked and ran and walked again. They felt as though a strong wind was blowing them on. It seemed as though it would blow them away with joy!

Earlier that afternoon, the wife of a gypsy pastor had brought these two women, a mother, and daughter, to me for prayer. They looked so depressed and oppressed and in terrible health. As I prayed, the Lord showed me I should take off some curses and then showed me which blessings to put in their place. As I ministered first to the daughter, she began to receive health. As I broke off a curse, she started to fall down in the spirit. (I quickly checked with the Lord to make sure if it was a devil or not, and it was not.) But it was interesting that when I went to catch her as she fell, she really didn't have any weight. I just guided her so that she would fall onto a couch. I believe there was an angel holding her up so she wouldn't get hurt when she went down! During that time, much deliverance happened to this young woman. Then I knew there was something going on

TURNING CURSES TO BLESSINGS

with the mother. I questioned her and she admitted that her son-in-law was abusing her daughter. She then went on to admit that her husband had also abused her! I told her that a generational curse had just been broken. She agreed, because she now had freedom instead of fear, and could talk about it for the first time. Then she said, "My mother and her mother also had abusing husbands." Then referring to her son-in-law, she said, "That man has hurt my daughter so much, I hate that man! I curse that man!"

Immediately I had to teach her that we are not to curse, but rather we are to bless. As soon as she realized it, she repented and tears fell. The whole atmosphere and situation changed. When the two women got ready to leave, I prayed for Momma again and this time **she** got complete deliverance from her past. It was a great time!

The key to these women getting delivered and receiving blessings was their repentance before God and their forgiveness of those who had cursed them. As soon as they were able to bless their husbands, God's blessings began to be poured out on both the mother and daughter. They were totally bowled over by all the peace, the joy, the healing, and the restoration—all in one package deal! They were obedient to forgive their husbands and they got the blessings. God is awesome and merciful! I was crying inside at the beginning as they painfully told me their stories. But when it was all over, I was ready to dance right out the door with them to celebrate all the blessings that were overtaking them.

God is our Father and the blessings He has reserved for His children are tremendous. All we need to do is open the gates of Heaven with obedience and forgiveness and faith, and He pours it all out on us.

THE BLESSINGS OF A FATHER

In Chapter 3, we saw how Abraham is our father of faith and his blessings are passed down to us, if we'll receive them. Now, to get on with the story, along came Abraham's grandsons, Isaac's twin sons. Their grandfather was dead and their father was already very old. Esau, the twin who was minutes older, was the firstborn. The boys (actually about seventy-six years old by then) got into a squabble about the inheritance. Jacob, the other twin, connived with his mother to make sure he got the blessings, instead of the older son. Here you have the sin of one parent loving one child more, and the other parent loving the other more. This brings into the bloodline a curse of division. The blessing of a Hebrew father for his first son is still very important, even to this day.

(Genesis 27:27-29) And he came near, and kissed him and Isaac smelled the smell of his raiment, and blessed him, and said,

TURNING CURSES TO BLESSINGS

See, the smell of my son is as the smell of a field which the LORD hath blessed:
Therefore God give thee of the dew of heaven, and the fatness of the earth, and plenty of corn and wine:
Let people serve thee, and nations bow down to thee: be lord over thy brethren, and let thy mother's sons bow down to thee: cursed be every one that curseth thee, and blessed be he that blesseth thee.

This blessing gave to Jacob the position of head of the family and protected him from the curses of others, as well as giving him all the blessings. Those are powerful words! And guess what? They were spoken to the wrong son. But Isaac had a problem; he favored one son over the other. Parents please don't favor one child over the others, because it is sin and it causes destruction. I have five children and none of them will ever tell you that I love one over the other. Loving one child over another is a sin and it brings curses upon you.

When I was a child, I learned this the hard way. I was abused, because my father didn't want me. I used to have so much pain that I would sneak away to my favorite place out on a hillside. In northern Minnesota during the day, when those clouds started moving, you could see every shape imaginable. At night, you could reach right up there and grab the stars of the Milky Way. One night at midnight, when I was about seven years old, I sneaked outside so my father wouldn't see me. My father's anger toward me hurt so bad that I didn't even want to live. I lay there and looked at those clouds and the stars and just prayed. God talked to me, as He often would do. I just looked up at the sky and said, "God, some day I want to be a daddy, but I don't want to be the kind I've got!" And God told me, "I have a lot of kids and I love them all the same. Do not ever favor one above another. Each of them has things that you can appreciate more and you encourage them in those things, but you love them all the same."

I've never forgotten that. He said one other thing, and that's my excuse for being childlike, "Never forget what it's like to be a kid!" At fifty-six years old, I can get down and play with the kids just as much as when I was six years old. Children are a great heritage.

Esau and Jacob had a problem because Esau was Daddy's favorite and Jacob was Momma's boy. This cost Momma her life and it caused all kinds of destructive things in their lives. This is an important thing that we have to watch carefully. The wrong son got the blessing because of deception, at Momma's suggestion. There are curses that come from deception. Deception won't pan out. It takes truth if you want to be blessed. If you are going to get the greatness of the blessings of God, you have to tell the truth.

There was not truth there. How did the younger son get the blessing? The older son was very selfish.

TURNING CURSES TO BLESSINGS

He sold his birthright for his belly's sake. He had set himself up. He had self-imposed curses. Self imposed curses are on the types of curses we need to deal with in our lives—our confession, the words we say. Have you ever heard anybody say, "Well, I'll be damned?" Whenever I hear anybody say that, I say, "No! No! Be blessed!"

Our words set us up for curses or blessings. Did you know that angels have no authority on this earth? Our words give them authority because we come from the dust of the earth, the "dirt connection," all the way to the heavenlies. There are two kinds of angels: God's heavenly angels and the devil's angels (those who fell by disobedience). They all listen to our words. We have the uniqueness of having the Spirit of God in us, so when we speak we have power. We're going to face judgment for all idle and evil words. We send out the devils against people, by speaking evil of them or even of ourselves. We say things like, "I'll never be able to do that," or "I'll never understand this."

James, the brother of Jesus, talks about the power of the tongue very clearly in the third chapter of the epistle.

(James 3:2-5) For in many things we offend all. If any man offend not in word, the same is a perfect man, and able also to bridle the whole body.

OVERFLOWING BLESSINGS

Behold, we put bits in the horses' mouths, that they may obey us; and we turn about their whole body.

Behold also the ships, which though they be so great, and are driven of fierce winds, yet are they turned about with a very small helm, whithersoever the governor listeth.

Even so the tongue is a little member, and boasteth great things. Behold, how great a matter a little fire kindleth!

I would admonish each of us that what comes out of our mouth is what is in our heart. The tongue is a little member, but it can bless or curse us.

(Genesis 27:33) And Isaac trembled very exceedingly, and said, Who? where is he that hath taken venison, and brought it me, and I have eaten of all before thou camest, and have blessed him? yea, and he shall be blessed.

It was very important for Esau and Jacob to get a blessing from their father in this situation, but the whole thing was set up for evil and to cause curses to come on people. It was a total set-up! Isaac realized that he had given the blessing to the wrong son. The father couldn't take back the blessings he had already given to Jacob. Did you know that blessings are irrevocable, that the only person who can revoke a blessing is the receiver? That's why, when someone says, "God bless you," it's there for eternity. Don't let go of it, and even more so if we say, "God bless you in the name of the Lord Jesus Christ!" It is a powerful thing. The same permanence occurs when a person speaks a curse on someone. If it's not dealt with, the curse stays there.

(Genesis 27:37) And Isaac answered and said unto Esau, Behold, I have made him thy lord, and all his brethren have I given to him for servants; and with corn and wine have I sustained him: and what shall I do now unto thee, my son?

A blessing means the giving of all. When God blesses you, He's giving you all His greatness. It's really interesting that the Father's blessing does not hold anything back. If you are not receiving God's blessing, it is because you're not doing faithfully what He says or you're not obeying, because God does not hold back.

(Genesis 27:38) And Esau said unto his father, Hast thou but one blessing, my father? Bless me, even me also, O my father. And Esau lifted up his voice, and wept.

OVERFLOWING BLESSINGS

Isaac didn't have anything more to give. He had given all the best to Jacob. That's why when someone says lightly, "Bless you, brother," I say, "Yeah, right." That's just like someone saying, "Merry Christmas," or "Excuse me." It's more than just a greeting or salutation. It's something that we have mutilated by not recognizing the greatness of it. Who do you think is behind that? Satan!

If you have been a victim as a child of being favored or not favored, it is necessary that you forgive your parents so the curse can hold no authority. If you are a parent and have been guilty of this, it is necessary to repent to God and then ask your children to forgive you also. And of course, you need to forgive yourself.

(Genesis 27:39, 40) And Isaac his father answered and said unto him, Behold, thy dwelling shall be the fatness of the earth, and of the dew of heaven from above;

And by thy sword shalt thou live, and shalt serve thy brother; and it shall come to pass when thou shalt have the dominion, that thou shalt break his yoke from off thy neck.

Esau's blessing was a curse. Isaac didn't have authority to bless him; he'd already given the blessing to Jacob. In his trying, he literally spoke a curse. When you try to bless someone with the wrong heart, you can literally curse him or her. It took a matter of about twenty years before these brothers got back together, and then it was very timidly. It had all started with deception and favoring one child above the other. It's amazing!

(Genesis 27:41) And Esau hated Jacob because of the blessing wherewith his father blessed him: and Esau said in his heart, The days of mourning for my father are at hand; then will I slay my brother Jacob.

Curses set up evil. Esau's father was a wonderful man and you would think he would be concerned and mourning for him. Esau literally didn't care what happened to his father. And because of the hatred that rose up in him, he was willing to commit murder. "As soon as they get done mourning him and all the traditional stuff that the church requires so they don't talk about me, then I'm going to kill my brother." Unforgiveness will cause death. It opens a door to more and more evil. Hollywood makes great movies of this. They portray the image that it is honorable to carry out vengeance. It is not honorable at all!

A very important key is that you remember to forgive the people who curse you. Forgiveness is everything and **we are responsible to forgive, whether people deserve it or not.** When we forgive, we're in God's grace and mercy and love. Of course,

OVERFLOWING BLESSINGS

some people don't deserve it. Did we deserve to be forgiven? No! But God sent His only-begotten Son to die on the cross so that you and I could be forgiven. It's a very important thing to get curses out of our lives. God sets things up so that we forgive, but it's not an easy thing to do. The more we forgive people, the more we appreciate what Jesus has done for us.

If you have areas of your life that are not under control, I would bet that you have a curse. And I'd also bet that when that curse is gone, your life will change. I know this for a fact, because I had curses on my own life and didn't even know it; I couldn't figure out why things didn't work out in my life. When the curses were removed, it made all the difference.

It is not my purpose to get everyone focused on curses to the point of fear, because this is not the heart of it. I do believe that when we expose the snare of the devil, the devil loses his power and we all want his power gone, right? That is the heart of this book and all the classes that I teach. It is to cause the devil to lose his power in your life and in my life. We can touch hundreds of people's lives with these simple keys and then we will see the devil's dominion being broken more fully. There is so much we can look forward to if we obey God. His blessings are overflowing and He is ready to pour them out at any time!

Back a few thousand years ago, there was a man named Moses who was God's friend and His servant. He was chosen to lead Jacob's descendants out of

TURNING CURSES TO BLESSINGS

Egypt. They were called Israelites after their great-great granddaddy. Did you know why God changed Jacob's name to Israel? Because God changed him from a cheat and a "supplanter" into a "prince with God." Jacob may have been very cursed, but the day came that he repented before God and asked Him for forgiveness. He also asked his brother Esau for forgiveness. Guess what? The curses were broken and God blessed him with tremendous blessings.

Moses finally got these people (three or four million of them) to the borders of the Promised Land, promised to them by God Himself. There he told them that on that day they would cross over the River Jordan. He told them that they would have to **take** the land. They would have to claim that which God promised them. We have a common thief that steals away our "land" (John 10:10). And we too have to make the good fight of faith for the promises of God.

(Deuteronomy 11:26) Behold, I set before you this day a blessing and a curse;

God reminds them of all the commands of God and then tells them all about the blessings they will receive if they obey God.

BLESSINGS WILL OVERTAKE YOU

(Deuteronomy 28:1) And it shall come to pass, if thou shalt hearken diligently unto

OVERFLOWING BLESSINGS

the voice of the LORD thy God, to observe and to do all his commandments which I command thee this day, that the LORD thy God will set thee on high above all nations of the earth:

God gives us responsibility. He says, "If thou shalt hearken diligently unto the voice of the LORD thy God." Only we can do this for ourselves. Then God says what he will do. He will set you on high above the nations. But this is only after the big "if" we do our part.

At one time, we in the United States were blessed, but we're not there anymore! Wake up America! Why do you think our country is faltering? Because we did not obey the voice of the Lord! I'm talking to Christians here. It is not the army that keeps the nation free. It is the obedience of God's people. The army is important, but it's the people of God who make it free. We did not listen to God's commandments diligently and now we're in big trouble!

(Deuteronomy 28:2) And all these blessings shall come on thee, and overtake thee, if thou shalt hearken unto the voice of the LORD thy God.

Do you know what? It's amazing to me that Christians are running everywhere looking for

TURNING CURSES TO BLESSINGS

blessings! Have you ever been "crying in your beer" because of things going wrong in your life? The key is that if you obey God's voice, blessings will overtake you—you won't have to look for them. All these blessings will overtake you; they'll catch up with you. When I was in high school, I liked to play football. I had a good arm and was fast on my feet, but the taller boys tried to overtake me. When you're overtaken, you can't get away! You can have the blessings so much that you can't get away from them.

In saying, "all these blessings shall overtake thee," to Israel, it was because they were His people. Today we as Christians are God's people and so we can have these same blessings overtake us. God took it from the nation to the individual, because the nation is made up of individuals. Now, there are only two nations I believe the Lord works with directly in this day: the nation called the **Body of Christ** and the nation called **marriage**, because a Christian marriage is to be the example to the Body of Christ and the world of our relationship one to another.

The Christian marriage is what raises up the next generation of the Body of Christ. One of the effects of a Christian marriage is that it stops the continuance of generational gaps. It is never God's will that we have a separation between the generations. Generational gaps are the fruit of sin in our homes and in our churches.

The Christian marriage and the Body of Christ are the two groups that God works with today. He does not work directly anymore with the nation called Israel like He did be in the Old Testament. He works with His people through the Body of Christ and through Christian marriage. Of course, He does work through single people because they are part of the Body of Christ.

Have you ever stopped to think why marriages receive such strong demonic attack? Just like the Body of Christ, attacks are relentless to keep people from seeking the Lord. They are relentless against the marriages to prevent the Word of God from being transplanted into future generations. I recently heard that Christian marriages passed the fifty percent mark in divorce rates. But when both the marriage and the Body of Christ put God first, then Christ can be the head in both and blessings will be the fruit.

(Deuteronomy 28:3) Blessed shalt thou be in the city, and blessed shalt thou be in the field.

The issue is not where we live, the issue is, are we blessed? If we were not, blessed it does not have to do with where we live, but whether we obey God.

(Deuteronomy 28:4) Blessed shall be the fruit of thy body,

What we have to do to get the blessings of God back in our children is to hearken diligently to the voice of the Lord our God and to obey His commandments. God is bigger than civil and national governments. We have a King whose name is Jesus and his nation is the Kingdom of God. This is the eternal nation. It is not falling apart; it's getting stronger. The fruit of your body can be blessed.

...and the fruit of thy ground,

Look at all the floods. We either have floods or droughts, floods or droughts! In the spring of 1998, the Red River Valley in northwest Minnesota flooded. My brother-in-law flew over it and discovered it had flooded to over forty miles wide! That's how bad the flood was, the distance from here to another city forty miles away! That's a big lake. This area is the breadbasket of the United States, big potato, and sugar beet country. Those aren't blessed fields, are they? What about the Mississippi Valley? They are having the five hundred year flood every other year!

...and the fruit of thy cattle, the increase of thy kine, and the flocks of thy sheep.

What about the mad cow disease? Such events are not without a cause, and they are not coincidental! Blessings from God flow because of obedience!

(Deuteronomy 28:5) Blessed shall be thy basket and thy store.

OVERFLOWING BLESSINGS

Cupboards full! Did you know that there was a time when America had enough food stored to feed the free world for two years? That was in the 1950's. Then the government came up with a program called "Soil Bank," in which they paid you not to farm. Now people are wondering what's going to happen in the year 2050!

(Deuteronomy 28:6) Blessed shalt thou be when thou comest in, and blessed shalt thou be when thou goest out.

Nobody knows whether they are coming or going anymore. It does not matter whether you're coming or going, you'll be blessed if you obey the Lord. That's awesome! Even if you don't know which way you're going, you'll still be blessed!

(Deuteronomy 28:7) The LORD shall cause thine enemies that rise up against thee to be smitten before thy face: they shall come out against thee one way, and flee before thee seven ways.

I love this! I used to be a fighter. If an enemy flees seven ways, it will have to be in seven pieces, two men in three and a half! What chance does your enemy have against you if you hearken unto the voice of the Lord your God? They don't stand a chance. We can

TURNING CURSES TO BLESSINGS

save America. It does not have anything to do with deserving it. God says that if we'll repent, He'll save the nation.

When I was in the Ukraine in 1994, the people who were our interpreters were of the communist government, whose bosses had changed their system. The government didn't need interpreters anymore. All of a sudden, these people were out of work. These were people with Ph.D.'s who knew English very well, because it was their job to infiltrate America. They came to me and said, "Russia is not disarming. They are still building a new submarine every month." (Now, their nuclear submarines are so silent that we can't detect them. They are still building them!) They asked me to talk to the President when I got back.

Do you know what? The leaders of our nation already know this. They are helping to break our nation. But, it's not the politicians that are going to save our land. If I'm stepping on your heroes, change heroes. I'm going to keep stepping. The Bible says I can step on his (the devil's) head! We can make our enemy flee. Honestly, we can turn around our nation so that we are blessed nation again. Get a picture of this! Get the picture: we can change things. Organizations are not the answer; they are just like another church. It's not the church; it's the people in the church, God's saints getting together. **We** can change this!

When we pray, God often puts his angels to work to make things happen. Have you ever seen an angel?

OVERFLOWING BLESSINGS

The closest that we have figured out is that there are about 30,000 angels per saint. I use mine and some of yours that you're not using! They hate unemployment. In America, we believe more in devil spirits than in angels. But it is the angels that are really impressive and the devil spirits that are just a joke.

Let me give you an example from something that happened in Romania. We had a foot washing in one of the communion services we did. It's not a religious thing. I'll tell you, if you have trouble with someone and can't get along with him, try washing his feet! Why do you think Jesus did that foot-washing experience with Peter in John 13:3-12? Because it took the arrogance out of Peter. It humbled him. It was a very humbling time. What we taught on in Romania was being worthy to receive communion. "Discerning the Lord's body" is not just picturing Jesus getting beat up for your healing. What it's talking about is that if I have a problem with you and I have bitterness towards you when I take communion, then I'm cursing myself. When I was done, the pastor told the people (about 250 of them) to get on their knees and repent so we could have communion, and boom! There were 250 people down on their knees repenting out loud. It sounded like a honeybee hive; it was so beautiful and productive. The Holy Spirit was in this because they were all talking and repenting and all of a sudden without any cue, everyone stopped talking.

TURNING CURSES TO BLESSINGS

As these people were on their knees repenting, all of a sudden I saw that the place was filling up with angels. As the people repented, the angels walked right over, cool and effortlessly, and grabbed devils. The devils were skinny and not very tall, distorted, twisted and ugly, biting and growling and kicking. They were doing everything they could to get loose, but the angels had them by the seat of their pants and by the nape of the neck and just walked out of the church with them. The devils could no longer hang on to the people because they had all repented of their sins!

So that I would not cause offense, I was not going to tell these people what I saw. The pastor turned to me and said, through the interpreter, "You have received a vision for this church and you'd better tell it." So, I told them what I saw. The faith of these people was strengthened and encouraged. Usually, after a meeting in a church that size there would be lines and lines of people standing to be ministered to, going on for two or three hours. This day only seven people came up for prayer, five of whom wanted prayer for their relatives! The rest had received their deliverance during the communion service.

That was the power of repentance! Those angels are there to serve us. It's quite an experience to see them at work. They have a ministry toward us in which we pray and they go out and do. We could pray something totally impossible, because to God all things are possible. Angels are ministering spirits sent

OVERFLOWING BLESSINGS

to minister to those who shall be heirs of salvation (Hebrews 11:14). They are our servants, there to carry out God's purposes in our lives. It's their job. They are the ones who can scatter your enemies in seven directions. They are the ones who can do things to cause submarines to bump into each other, to blow up, or whatever it would take to stop our enemies. We're talking about war and war is not friendly. I'm not a terrorist. If I didn't have Jesus, I'd be a terrorist and I wouldn't blow up buildings. I'd blow up people! Praise God, I don't do those things, but I do understand the reality of warfare. When you have an enemy, you have to come on full force. God has made available to us seven times more protection over the size of the enemy coming at us.

Unfortunately, there are people who just can't accept the blessings God has for them. One time I was ministering healing to the associate pastor of a Pentecostal Church and he started getting healed. He started getting new bodily parts put in, because his intestines had been taken out and all he had left was a sack. He felt new organs being put in, and even commented to the Senior Pastor that he could feel them being put in. He felt the heat but as soon as I took out a spirit of infirmity, I was kicked out of the church. In this particular brand of church, they do not believe that any Christian can have devil spirits. All of a sudden, doctrine had become more important than deliverance. The man lost his healing as a result.

TURNING CURSES TO BLESSINGS

(Deuteronomy 28:8) The LORD shall command the blessing upon thee in thy storehouses, and in all that thou settest thine hand unto; and he shall bless thee in the land which the LORD thy God giveth thee.

When God commands something, you can't stop it. Right now, America's food surplus is just a few weeks. If you don't have some extra rice and beans stashed away, just a scare would cause everything to be grabbed up quickly. The warehouses would be out of food quickly. I'm not saying this to scare you. Wake up, America! It's not a sin to be prepared. Joseph took all the wealth of Egypt of the day and prepared it for the children of Israel.

(Deuteronomy 28:9) The LORD shall establish thee an holy people unto himself, as he hath sworn unto thee, if thou shalt keep the commandments of the LORD thy God, and walk in his ways.

If we obey God's commandments, God will establish us. Do you know what it means for God to establish you? There could be a whole army coming after just you and they would not succeed. He can cause nuclear warheads to turn around and go back to where they came from, like a homing pigeon does! We don't have a problem, if we do what God wants. If we won't obey, we'll have a big problem.

(Deuteronomy 28:10) And all people of the earth shall see that thou art called by the name of the LORD; and they shall be afraid of thee.

The people of the United States of America, used to be greatly blessed. Other nations feared us. We have authority in the name of the Lord and need to use it. Now other countries are making fun of us. I travel on a lot of airplanes. Do you know what I do when I get on one? I walk down the ramp and before I get on the airplane I say, "God bless you, airplane, in the name of Jesus Christ!" There's power in that. I had a stewardess tell the pilot what I had done and then he came back to where I was sitting, shook hands with me and said, "God bless you, sir. Thank you. I've never had anyone bless this airplane."

If you say, "God bless you," you'd better mean it and expect to have it. When you obey the voice of the Lord your God, you have authority. When I pray for you and say, "God bless you," guess what happens? God assigns angels and whatever else it takes to work so you will be God-blessed. It's not because of our greatness; it's because of the power of Christ in us, the hope of glory. It's something very real. It's the same when you tell me that God may bless me. I'd love to see this nation get to the point where all the

TURNING CURSES TO BLESSINGS

people of the earth shall see that we are called by the name of the Lord.

(Deuteronomy 28:11) And the LORD shall make thee plenteous in goods, in the fruit of thy body, and in the fruit of thy cattle, and in the fruit of thy ground, in the land which the LORD sware unto thy fathers to give thee.

Israel was an agricultural society. But this could be interpreted for our time, to bless our work and our businesses. And, instead of our children being a cursed generation, they could be a blessed generation, and continue to serve God.

(Deuteronomy 28:12) The LORD shall open unto thee his good treasure, the heaven to give the rain unto thy land in his season, and to bless all the work of thine hand: and thou shalt lend unto many nations, and thou shalt not borrow.

You see, if you hearken unto the voice of the Lord your God, He shall do it! He takes upon Himself this responsibility. America is so indebted that the American dollar has very little value overseas anymore.

When we were in Amsterdam on our way back from India, we had nine hours to wait in the airport for our flight out to the USA. After twelve hours of travel from India, we were looking forward to going to a restaurant and having something good to eat for breakfast. We shopped around and they were charging $30 to $40 dollars just for a breakfast of eggs, sausage, and toast. Now is the time we should be considering investing in God's work before the dollar loses its value totally, unless we have a big turnaround.

When our nation stood on godly standards, we lent and did not borrow. Now our nation is so indebted that the farmland is owned by foreigners, the manufacturing, the oil, and most of the things that belonged to Americans are now owned by foreign investors.

(Deuteronomy 28:13) And the LORD shall make thee the head, and not the tail; and thou shalt be above only, and thou shalt not be beneath; if that thou hearken unto the commandments of the LORD thy God, which I command thee this day, to observe and to do them:

I like this verse! I have a T-shirt at home showing a dogsled in Alaska and it is captioned: "The scenery is great in Alaska—as long as you're the lead dog!" Guess what the second and third dogs get to look at? God will make obedient people into being the head, not the tail!

TURNING CURSES TO BLESSINGS

(Deuteronomy 28:14) And thou shalt not go aside from any of the words which I command thee this day, to the right hand, or to the left, to go after other gods to serve them.

This is what is happening in America today! How much clearer could it be? You might say, "Well, but you're reading in the Old Testament." I can find every one of these things in the Church epistles, and so can you. What we need to do is to obey God and repent, and His blessings will overtake us.

After Moses told the Israelites about God's commandments and the rewards, or blessings, for obeying them, he went on to tell them what would happen if they disobeyed God. Then he instructed them that after they crossed over the Jordan River into the land of promise, they were to have a very serious ceremony. God set it up so the people would never forget. (That's what ceremonies are all about. We have weddings so the vows and the pictures and the witnesses will all remind us that we made some very serious promises to our husbands or wives. It's also good for the kids. They look at our photo albums and recognize something much more important than just a birthday bash.)

On that day, God told the children of Israel that half of them were to stand on Mount Gerizim and call out God's blessings. Then, on the other side of the valley, on Mount Ebal, the other half of the Israelites

OVERFLOWING BLESSINGS

were to stand and call out the curses from God for not obeying His commands. Can you imagine what that must have been like? A million and a half, or two, people calling out blessings and over yonder, another one and a half or two million calling back with the curses? Man, if I had been there I'd never have forgotten that day! I would have thought twice before I disobeyed the commands of God. Don't you think that if our children heard even two hundred of us on one side of a gully and two hundred on the other responding, that they'd take us a lot more seriously? God loves to bless us, but He is not to be mocked. He is serious about it. We had better get serious, so we don't get cursed by God Himself!

Chapter 5
Does God Curse?

One night I was teaching in a church that did not believe that people legitimately fall down under the power of the Holy Spirit. Now, I'm not into knocking people down when I pray for them, like I've seen some preachers do. In fact, I used to hold them up and would hurt my back doing so, just so they wouldn't fall down. Since I don't want to offend anybody, I'm always very careful with people when I pray for them. I just make sure it's not a devil putting them down. The power is not in the manifestation of God's Spirit; the power is in the name of Jesus.

As soon as I finished teaching, I asked for people to come to the front if they wanted prayer for anything. The girl almost ran up to us and so we prayed for her. Boom—she was on the floor! We couldn't have held her up if we tried. So, I just put an angel with her and said, "Who's next?" but nobody would come up for prayer, because in that particular group, if someone fell under the Spirit, they thought it was a devil. So I said, "That's good. You're giving me an easy day. Usually I have to go on for hours. Thank you. God bless you. Good-bye."

I was taking my time to pack up everything. Then I said to them, "If it's from God, the fruit will be good." I kept packing up calmly and nobody was saying anything nor coming up for prayer. The retarded girl started to laugh. Her laughter was so contagious. It flowed from deep inside her, as though

TURNING CURSES TO BLESSINGS

something was coming loose. Pretty soon, everybody was laughing, even a little five-month-old baby in its mother's arms. There on the carpeted floor lay the young retarded woman, laughing her heart out for forty-five minutes!

The whole church began laughing with her. I said, "Is there anyone short of joy in this room, lacking the good fruit?" Everyone became free from their inhibitions and began to come up front for prayer. After the forty-five minutes she was down, when the retarded girl got up, she had a totally sound mind. The curses had been removed from her life.

You see, there's no limit to what God can do! We limit God. I could see that she and God had something going on, so I was getting out of the way. I just left it alone. Did God curse her? What kind of curses did she have on her life?

CAUSES FOR CURSES FROM GOD

In this chapter, we are going to see different things that we do to bring curses directly from God. Yes, God does curse. It is not blasphemy to say that God curses. The problem is that we all know better than God. Look at what He says through the prophet.

(Malachi 2:2) If ye will not hear, and if ye will not lay it to heart, to give glory unto my name, saith the LORD of hosts, I will even send a curse upon you, and I will curse your

DOES GOD CURSE?

blessings: yea, I have cursed them already, because ye do not lay it to heart.

One source of curses comes from unintentionally spoken words. God is not playing games with us. We can't just play church. If we hear the word of the Lord and don't obey it and give the glory to Him, every time we say, "God bless you," we're cursing someone. Think about it. What about someone you know that's not honoring God with his life, but blesses you? You'd better watch out, he's really cursing you according to Malachi 2:2. This is what can be called a clergy curse.

Did you know that clergymen could curse you? If you don't believe the way they do, lots of times they get angry and tell you you're listening to Satan rather than God. What about a preacher who is homosexual or who is an adulterer and officiates at a young couple's wedding? He pronounces a "blessing" over the two, but God says that's really a curse. Have you ever been cursed by a priest or by a preacher? If you have, be sure to forgive him or her, break off the curse, and ask God to fill you with blessings instead.

There's also the case of those ministers who get puffed up with what they are doing and take for themselves the glory that God deserves. Those people are cursed by God.

This is the reason I don't let a lot of people pray for me. First, we hear and then we take it to heart. Only then can we give God the glory. Another source of curses is not giving glory to God, substituting idols instead.

(Deuteronomy 27:15) Cursed be the man that maketh any graven or molten image, an abomination unto the LORD, the work of the hands of the craftsman, and putteth it in a secret place. And all the people shall answer and say, Amen.

I used to live around cursed statues in New Mexico. In the 1540's, the Roman Catholic Church came right up to where my house was. The street we lived on was part of the old Camino Real, the oldest street in America. White men settled New Mexico long before either coast. They came up to plunder and to take the riches, and they brought in many graven images. Of course, the Indians already had a lot of them, so they just mixed them up and had image stew.

Idols are not necessarily just little statues. A person's job could be your idol. A person could be saying, "I'm not going to change. I'm going to stay the way I am." Property could be an idol. It could be all kinds of things. False gods will definitely bring curses into one's life. When the Bible says, "Do something," people need to do it even if they don't feel like it. God can start changing their heart.

I love the United States of America and its flag, but our allegiance has to be with God and not with a symbol. I believe that the American flag has become an idol. It is an image that is worshipped by many people in the United States. This is idolatry. The pledge of allegiance the children say every day in school is idolatry. They pledge their allegiance to a flag, as well as to the country. I'm sorry, but my only allegiance is to the Lord God Almighty and I don't believe in singing songs to a flag and making pledges to it. Why? Because God says, we're not to have images. Do you know how the pledge to the flag was put into the public schools? A phrase was added just to keep the Christians happy, "one nation under God." That phrase was not in the original version. As a concession they put that in, but then prayer was prohibited a few years later.

Many people call the work of the hands of a craftsman, "art," and we justify keeping our idols this way. What we call art is really graven images and these defile our homes and churches. We will discuss more in a later chapter about cursed objects.

(Deuteronomy 27:16) Cursed be he that setteth light by his father or his mother. And all the people shall say, Amen.

The Word of God says to treat your parents with respect. It says, "Honor your father and mother," in Ephesians 6, and if you're not doing so, you are cursed. I don't care how bad your parents may or may not have been; the Bible says, "Honor them." It's not your business to judge your parents. You are to

TURNING CURSES TO BLESSINGS

respect them. Not giving them respect is a cause for being cursed by God.

We're living in a generation that is so cursed. One reason why is that, parents of this generation have removed themselves so far from God and the things of God. Parents have not prayed and given thanks over meals. They have not eaten together as a family, prayed together, or strived to do what is right. They have let the television baby-sit our children. Because they have not taught their children about sex, and what's right and honorable, the schools took on this job. The public school has not taught abstinence but has taught birth control and "safe sex." Many times the parents do not have the right to know that their daughters are having an abortion. The spiritual reason for such actions by the schools is because parents failed to do the things of God. They lost their rights as parents. The parents are not right all the time, but the children need to honor their parents anyway.

Do you know what our children are being taught in public schools, moms, and dads? Some people at the church I was pastoring were all upset one day. They brought me a quiz paper from their fourth grade child. One of the questions on the quiz was, "What does your father think of homosexuality?" That little child, by obeying the teacher and telling the truth, saying that his dad did not like it, got cursed. The child's family values were recorded. You see, ungodly governments want to make Christianity illegal.

DOES GOD CURSE?

I would hope that Christians are bold enough in their communities to be fully identifiable even without having to question anybody! I hope there's enough evidence against you that you'll get arrested, because Jesus will still get you out. You'll have earthquakes in the prison, if necessary, to get you free. Parents, if you're not teaching your children to respect their parents, you're setting your kids up to be cursed and the generations following. Get serious! This does not point kindly at America.

(Deuteronomy 27:17) Cursed be he that removeth his neighbour's landmark. And all the people shall say, Amen.

Removing boundary markers is cheating, stealing, and robbing. Israelite landmarks consisted of piles of stones at each corner of their land to show it was theirs. If the neighbor was gone for a while, you could move the stones a few feet to gain a few feet, but you'd be cursed for it. That is stealing someone's land. In that day and time, it was a big issue because this was an inheritance from God.

Even now, it still is a big deal to cheat and steal. Some say, "Oh, well, they won't know the difference." Someone accidentally gives you five dollars too much change. I'll guarantee you, you'll be blessed if you are honest and take the five dollars back. How about just lying about somebody to get a job promotion because you're next in line? These are the kinds of offenses that bring curses from God.

In 1967, Israel went to war. God restored back the land to Israel through many awesome miracles. Israel was totally outnumbered and outgunned, outclassed and disadvantaged. God gave them a great victory in six days and restored all the land that had been withheld from them. Yet, now, in 1999, they are negotiating to give it back to the enemy. I believe that this is "removing their neighbor's landmark." Through this, Israel and all nations involved in this, are setting themselves up to be cursed by God.

(Deuteronomy 27:18) Cursed be he that maketh the blind to wander out of the way. And all the people shall say, Amen.

We'd better never get in the way of a disadvantaged person or of a child when they are looking for God. This is a serious offense and brings curses directly from God. God has a special tender place in His heart for the disabled and the very young, and He blesses those who bless them and curses those who curse them. When I was a kid, we had "harelip jokes" about people who were born with cleft palates and couldn't pronounce their words clearly. We laughed at them. We were cursing ourselves. How do you think those poor people with harelips felt?

Deuteronomy 27:18 is talking about the blind people who are used to walking, and they know how

DOES GOD CURSE?

many steps to take. But someone moves an object over so they fall and everybody laughs. This verse includes the idea of not wanting to have anything to do with someone because they are strange, they quiver, and they twitch due to physical impairments. Don't have anything to do with such people who mock and deride those people who are less fortunate. Go ahead and take the curse. In fact, you are blessed if you take in the undesirables.

Guess where Jesus would go? Do you think he would go where there were plush red carpets and leather seats? He'd pass that right by if the love of God were not there. He'd go right down to Joe's Bar and Grill. That's where he was needed. He could go down and get those people out of there. He'd go down to the insane asylum. That's one reason why I believe Jesus was blessed. I believe Jesus was always blessed for doing the will of his Father, and Jesus did not cause the blind to wander out of the way. He healed them.

(Deuteronomy 27:19) Cursed be he that perverteth the judgment of the stranger, fatherless, and widow. And all the people shall say, Amen.

One time I saw a policeman run through a red light and hit a car, then turn on his light. Someone came over and told him, "Well, the light really was green for you." He had turned on his light so it would look like he had come for the emergency, and the man who was innocent would get blamed for it. I ran right over there and I said, "I saw what happened," because the policeman went through the red light. If it had been the other way around, I would have done the same thing, because I do not believe in manipulation and lying, and I don't want to be cursed.

Turning your back on people with needs is probably the most common way of perverting judgment. Regarding the man who sits on the corner and asks for money, people say, "They bring him here in the morning before the sun comes up in a Mercedes! He does not really need help!" Have you ever heard that kind of statement? When you see a poor person begging, why not ask the Lord whether you should help him. I lived in the Sun Belt, where there are a lot of people who beg. Some of them deserve to be there and some of them probably even deserve to be imprisoned for being rapists and murderers on the run. But I'm not the judge. If the Lord tells me to help them, and I don't obey right away, then I have to turn around and drive back. Sometimes I probably don't hear Him, but people are needy and we **do** have to help.

(Deuteronomy 27:20) Cursed be he that lieth with his father's wife; because he uncovereth his father's skirt. And all the people shall say, Amen.

DOES GOD CURSE?

This is incest. It might not necessarily be the mother. It could be the step-mom, but it's still incest. Incest will bring curses every time, and they'll go on for generations and generations. I know, because recently the Lord directed me to remove a curse in the name of Jesus that had been there from eighteen generations before, when there had been incest. This is really bad stuff! It's no wonder the devil wants to get people to do it!

(Deuteronomy 27:21) Cursed be he that lieth with any manner of beast. And all the people shall say, Amen.

Did you know that people involved in black magic are having sex with the animals? Then they sacrifice the animal and after identifying where the Christians live, they take the blood and wipe it on their mailboxes to curse their communication. I've had people call up and ask me, "What are we going to do about it?" First of all, just wash it off with soap and water and then anoint it with oil and pray. The enemy is very sincere. Do you know what? You can't afford to hang around with fornication, adultery, and pornography anymore. Because the devil is going right down real soon and you could go down with him. He's not your friend. He wants you dead.

(Deuteronomy 27:22) Cursed be he that lieth with his sister, the daughter of his

father, or the daughter of his mother. And all the people shall say, Amen.

Here again is incest. What we do in our society is to say, "Well, we'll just abort the fetus." That brings a curse of innocent blood. This is serious stuff. This brings curses from God Himself.

(Deuteronomy 27:23) Cursed be he that lieth with his mother in law. And all the people shall say, Amen.

Most guys can't get along with their mother-in-law, but doing this (having sex with her) is incest.

(Deuteronomy 27:24) Cursed be he that smiteth his neighbour secretly. And all the people shall say, Amen.

This verse refers to hitting, striking, causing harm or any kind of grief in secret. You're not to set things up to cause your neighbor harm. Who are your neighbors? The people around you are your neighbors. They are the people that you have the best opportunity to bless and to introduce to the Lord Jesus Christ.

This also refers to taking advantage of your neighbor (like the case of moving his landmark), and includes all kinds of deceitful things. Just manipulating and taking advantage of your neighbor brings a curse on you. One of the things that I see happens sometimes to people who open their homes to meet for Bible study and prayer is that rumors are spread around the neighborhood to defame them. The people who do it are actually cursing themselves. A caution to those of you who open your house up for worship and those of you who attend: make sure you pray for protection on those homes. The devil is serious, but then, so are we!

(Deuteronomy 27:25) Cursed be he that taketh reward to slay an innocent person. And all the people shall say, Amen.

Of course, this is talking about hit men, paid assassins. It's not just the Mafia types that are doing it now. We've seen kids do it for others who want to get rid of their parents, or as rites of passage into satanic cults. They are in big trouble, not just with the law but with God also.

This verse also includes taking a bribe to condemn someone with his or her testimony. "Yes, I'll lie in court. I'll say that he didn't have any brake lights" when somebody rear-ends somebody. That kind of thing is going to bring curses. And the sad thing about curses is that they don't stop with you, unless you don't have any generations to follow you. Also, not having any generations to follow you is a curse.

TURNING CURSES TO BLESSINGS

(Deuteronomy 27:26) Cursed be he that confirmeth not all the words of this law to do them. And all the people shall say, Amen.

The purpose of the law was to keep people from going under curses. Grace is given for the same reason. It's not an excuse to do evil. Do you know what the answer of the law was if you did something that brought a curse? Death. Then you didn't have any generations to follow. See, Jesus hadn't been hung on the tree yet. The answer to getting rid of a curse now is death too, but it is the death of Jesus. He paid an awful debt and He didn't deserve it. He didn't deserve it at all and He did it so you and I could have our lives cleaned up and we could be thankful. The bottom line is still that the only difference between you and the people back in Deuteronomy is that you are bought by the blood of Jesus. It took His blood spilling to overcome sin. It was Jesus' blood, not the blood of bulls and goats, like in the Old Testament! Now you think about that!

I do not promote making people afraid of being left behind (when Jesus comes again for his people) and all these things, to keep them from sinning. I promote what I believe God would have me to promote, and that is that your love relationship with God and Jesus be so great that your reason for not sinning is not because of the consequences. How about if your reason for not sinning is because you hate sin? Is not that more powerful than being afraid of the consequences of sin? The more we love God, the more we will hate sin.

This doctrine of being afraid of the consequences of sin is a near hit. Have you ever been hunting and lost the animal because of a near hit, in which you hit a stump or just wounded the animal or something like that? It should be a bull's eye! That's what God wants, for you to be on target. And on target is that we quit sinning because our love for the Lord is so great that we hate sin! We should see sin as mocking Jesus who gave it all. That's how we can live free from curses.

CURSED BY TRUSTING IN MAN

(Jeremiah 17:5) Thus saith the LORD; Cursed be the man that trusteth in man, and maketh flesh his arm, and whose heart departeth from the LORD.

This verse is one that controlling governments do not like. They want us to depend on the government and its programs. I am not a political guy, nor am I either Republican or Democrat. I am a monarchist. I have a King whose name is Jesus, and that's what motivates me. It's not the politics, the handout I can get, and the freebies. Some people think they need it, but they don't need it. They've been caught in a trap!

Our whole governmental system is set up for us to depend on man. The whole system is set up so that

TURNING CURSES TO BLESSINGS

people will be cursed! Isn't that something? From the womb to the tomb, our government wants to take care of us. I don't trust them: I trust in the Lord! The Bible says:

(Proverbs 3:5, 6) Trust in the Lord with all your heart. Lean not on your own understanding;
In all your ways acknowledge Him and He will direct your paths.

People are always going around saying, "I don't know what to do!" One reason is because they don't trust the Lord.

Socialistic programs and handouts make you cursed! I was not the one to say it—I just finished reading it! The Lord said it! We need to be at the point where our dependency is on the Lord Jesus Christ, so that when we come together, as in a church building, then we have power. That way, when someone comes in sick, they leave well. We in the church, the Body of Christ, have let ourselves become cursed because we've trusted in man. We say, "The pastor gets a salary. Let him do it," or, "I'm not an evangelist; I don't have to witness!" Where is that in the Bible? It must be one of those new versions. You know, the pastor needs your help.

I believe there are many pastors who could go out in the world and be a great success because they are very talented and capable men. I know that every pastor desperately (unfortunately, I have to say "desperately") needs people who are willing to get the job done, to pitch in and do. Praise God, I see a lot of healthy things in some churches, and one of them is the involvement of the people. This is a powerful thing. That's what you need to do and quit trusting in man.

(Jeremiah 17:7-8) Blessed is the man that trusteth in the LORD, and whose hope the LORD is.
For he shall be as a tree planted by the waters, and that spreadeth out her roots by the river, and shall not see when heat cometh, but her leaf shall be green; and shall not be careful in the year of drought, neither shall cease from yielding fruit.

I used to live in desert country, and would see trees that were all nice and green on the Rio Grande. They never had to be watered, or anything. They were taken care of. That is how God takes care of us if we obey His word.

Christians should be like that tree planted by the water. We don't have to worry about who is elected or who is not elected, or any of these things. We need to be spreading out our roots by the river, that regardless what drought comes, our roots are right down there in the aquifer! We are watered by the Holy Spirit. That's where Christians should be, regardless of where we live. That's where the Lord wants us to be and if we're not there, then we're missing something.

The prophet Zechariah was given a vision to show us another curse from God.

(Zechariah 5:1-4) Then I turned, and lifted up mine eyes, and looked, and behold a flying roll.

And he said unto me, What seest thou? And I answered, I see a flying roll; the length thereof is twenty cubits, and the breadth thereof ten cubits.

Then said he unto me, This is the curse that goeth forth over the face of the whole earth: for every one that stealeth shall be cut off as on this side according to it; and every one that sweareth shall be cut off as on that side according to it.

I will bring it forth, saith the LORD of hosts, and it shall enter into the house of the thief, and into the house of him that sweareth falsely by my name: and it shall remain in the midst of his house, and shall consume it with the timber thereof and the stones thereof.

God speaks to this prophet thousands of years ago and what He says is still true. Those who steal, those who swear an oath, those who give false testimony after swearing in court on a Bible, all these

DOES GOD CURSE?

people are cursed. This curse goes into their house, their family, and there it remains. In the old days, the house meant all the family and their descendents, such as in "the house of Israel," or "the house of Jacob." What's it talking about? That's talking about generations, is it not? And these are curses coming from God! Don't you think it was a curse that people didn't get on the boat in Noah's time? All over the face of the earth, people were doing these things.

Don't think that just because this curse was given thousands of years ago, you can say, "Oh, but now we're under God's grace." Then we trust grace so we can go out and sin and use it as an excuse. Later, we "cry in our beer" because of all the grief we have in our life.

If you get rid of the things that cause the grief, you can be delivered. We have seen hundreds of people delivered of all kinds of things, cancer, business failure, broken marriages, blind eyes—I can't possibly remember them all. The wages of sin is death. We need to sharpen up on what causes curses. Just because this is the grace administration, we just can't do whatever we please. Stealing and lying and perjuring bring curses.

CURSES FROM MEN ON GOD'S BEHALF

Let's talk about curses from men on God's behalf. Do you know why people kill prophets? Because the prophets say, "change or die," and people get mad. Praise God that they come and warn you! Sometimes as a prophet, you have to speak a message from God that people don't always want to hear. From Joshua 6, I'm going to show you a curse brought by a man of God. He spoke it on God's behalf.

(Joshua 6:26) And Joshua adjured them at that time, saying, Cursed be the man before the LORD, that riseth up and buildeth this city Jericho: he shall lay the foundation thereof in his firstborn, and in his youngest son shall he set up the gates of it.

The city of Jericho was the next obstacle they had to confront after crossing the flooded Jordan into the Promised Land. It was a city so powerful that with most of our weapons we have today we still couldn't get in. The wall around the city was built at a sharp angle; historians claim it was about 60 feet high and 40 feet wide. It was wide at the bottom and narrowed towards the top. If you were to hit it with a tank, the tank would roll over. There was nothing you could do; it was a sharp enough grade. It had a wall that was impossible to climb, but the amazing thing about it was that above, on top of the wall was a freeway going around it. It was forty feet wide all the way around that city! If you sent all your troops in on the North side to take it, they could move all their troops and get them there before you could bring down the

DOES GOD CURSE?

wall. They could rush their army, including chariots, to any part of the wall where the attack came from. They would bring in hot oil, or anything else they needed, to dump over the side onto the aggressor. It was solid wall. They didn't have cannon balls in those days, but if they had, they would have just ricocheted off the walls. There was absolutely no way that Jericho could be destroyed. There was no way they could break down the walls.

And yet, do you know what brought these defenses down? God! He did it in a way that proved that only He could do it! The Israelites obeyed God and marched around for seven days. And on the last day, they blasted their trumpets and shouted praises to the Lord and the walls came tumbling down. Do you know why we always have praise time at the beginning of any of our meetings? It's because **praise brings down the walls.** The Israelites obeyed and praised and brought down the entire city wall. They destroyed that city, the total city, except for the house of Rahab and her family. Everything else was destroyed by praise. Those of you who are prayer warriors and intercessors and are getting beat up and worn out, spend a little more time praising. Your intercession time will be shorter. It's a powerful thing!

God did a mighty act and it was to be an example. He had finally brought his people into the Promised Land and He wanted that heap of rubble in Jericho to remind the people who was Boss. Was it good real estate? You bet! It had the view; it had fresh water and everything that a developer would want. It was prime real estate! But Joshua went and told them, "Don't develop this property because if you do, if you lay the foundation down, your firstborn is going to die."

In that culture, to lose your firstborn son was a serious thing, and this prophecy added that they would also lose their youngest son when they put on the gates.

(1 Kings 16:34) In his days did Hiel the Bethelite build Jericho: he laid the foundation thereof in Abiram his firstborn, and set up the gates thereof in his youngest son Segub, according to the word of the LORD, which he spake by Joshua the son of Nun.

One day a man called Hiel decided to rebuild Jericho in direct disobedience to Joshua's prophecy. This man's pride and disobedience to the word of God caused him to lose his oldest son. It was a curse to lose your oldest son, your inheritor. Hiel should at least have been smart enough to stop his project once he laid the foundation and lost his firstborn. You'd think that he would have called the general contractor and said, "Hey, listen, we're going to have to stop building right now."

The curse happened and it happened from disobedience. "Oh, but God is love; He would never

DOES GOD CURSE?

do that." Oh, yeah? How do you explain this, folks? We have an awesome God. He does not go for mockery! When I think about Elijah, who went to the leadership of his nation and said, "Change or else," they didn't, so they went into a drought that destroyed them. When the Word of God speaks it is going to happen. It does not do us any good to disobey and say it can't happen. It's going to happen! And you can say, "Well, God is awfully hard." But, do you know what? The ruins of Jericho are the greatest example to mankind of the power of God coming up against the greatness of man. That's why God said not to rebuild it. But Hiel did it anyway and he was warned not to do it.

This is why we get into so much trouble. We're going to do it in the way we want to do it and don't listen to what anybody else has to say. After all, we say, "Hey, I'm a king, I'm a master builder. I have a license to build this city. And I'm the union contractor." It didn't do Hiel any good.

Hiel probably felt he was doing all right because his king was Ahab. "And Ahab did more to provoke the Lord God of Israel to anger than all the kings of Israel that were before him" (1 Kings 16:33). Ahab ended up getting his justice, too, as we see in the rest of this account in I Kings.

(1 Kings 17:1) And Elijah the Tishbite, who was of the inhabitants of Gilead, said unto Ahab, As the LORD God of Israel

TURNING CURSES TO BLESSINGS

liveth, before whom I stand, there shall not be dew nor rain these years, but according to my word.

If Ahab had been meek to the man of God, the prophet, if he had been meek to what God had told him to do, this curse would not have happened. But the whole nation suffered because of this curse. For three years and six months, there was not a drop of rain, not even a sprinkle. People starved to death; the nation crumbled because they were an agricultural society. They couldn't have C-130's (transport airplanes) bring in food from other nations—they were in trouble! If Ahab had been meek, the curse would not have happened.

We have seen how disobedience causes curses to come from God. Because he is a just God, he cannot reward disobedience. But he causes blessings on our behalf when we obey.

Chapter 6
Innocent Blood

We had been ministering in a church in Bucharest until about eleven at night and after the service was over, a gypsy pastor came up to me and said, "You must come with me." And I said, "Well, where?" He answered, "To my village." So I told him I could come tomorrow night. He promised to send someone to get us the next evening. The next night they came with a rickety old Dacha and we set off for the village. It seemed as if we'd fall out in the street every time the car hit a bump.

When we arrived, there were only fifteen people present. The pastor apologized and said, "I'm sorry this is all we are. Americans won't usually come unless there's a big crowd." I replied, "Jesus would stop for just one, so we'd better too. But the night is beautiful. Let's have church outside."

"We never thought of doing that," responded the gypsy pastor. They got their instruments together, and they certainly have some wild instruments! If you ever have a chance to go to a gypsy church, do it! If you have any trouble raising your hands and praising God, you won't be able to stay sitting. The worship service is not out of control. It's just that there's so much love for the Lord, you'll start feeling it down to the tips of your toes.

It was a powerful time. The music began to draw others from the neighborhood. They wanted to see what was going on. Because we were the only show in

TURNING CURSES TO BLESSINGS

town, everybody in the whole town showed up. Spiritually, I could feel a kind of electricity in the air. About three hundred people gathered, all packed into the tiny churchyard. They also spilled into the street around, then into the field next door, all exuberantly waving their arms. The praise music and the novelty of white-skinned American speakers made quite an attraction. They had come out of curiosity. But then the Holy Spirit began to move.

The Lord said to me: "Read Psalm 109 to them regarding the curse that was put on Judas Iscariot and his heirs. Tell them that they are cursed and that this is the curse upon them." I started thinking, "Well, this is impossible, because it says that Judas' name will be blotted out in the next generation." But the Lord told me unmistakably, "That's talking about the males. The women change their name when they get married." I didn't understand much at all about this, but I figured that the Lord knew what he was doing. So I showed the interpreter the part I wanted read in Romanian.

The people became dead serious by then, because the gypsies are very knowledgeable about curses. They are always being cursed because of their lifestyle. Then I said, "Those of you who want to be freed of this curse, raise your right hand." It was dusk in the little gypsy village and a bit hard to see, but we could make out lots of hands up and waving. They all raised their right hands because no one wanted to be left out. We could see the silhouettes of their hands up. I told them not to put their hands down until we

INNOCENT BLOOD

finished praying. We broke the power of that curse over them in the name of the Lord Jesus.

There were so many people there who did not know the Lord Jesus and the message flowed regarding salvation. "Jesus is the one who died and paid the price for you, to set you free. He died on the cross, but God raised Him from the dead!"

Then I said, "Those of you who want to know this Jesus who has freed you from your curses and to make Jesus Lord of your life, raise both arms and hold them up and don't put them down." Every hand, as nearly as I could tell, was up and when I prayed, three hundred to four hundred people came to the Lord Jesus that night. When I said, "Amen," they all started moving up to encircle us and to touch us. The love of God was overflowing and we kept saying, "God bless you, God bless you, God bless you!" It was one of the most moving times of my whole life. I had read Psalm 109 many times and had thought about how Jesus' heart must have hurt as he was sitting there that night at the last supper. He knew the Bible well and by then, he knew that Psalm 109 was a prophecy about Judas. You can imagine the heaviness He felt because He loved Judas. I had read this Psalm and had felt the hurt, but never realized until the Lord told me, that it pertained to the gypsies.

Did it make any difference for the people in that village, having the curses removed? It sure did! Many villagers received healing in their bodies, as a result. They were freed from oppression and depression and many other things. I found out the following year that from that simple meeting, about a hundred churches sprang up.

There are some wonderful pastors who have taken the chance and had the audacity to work with the gypsies despite the adverse pressure from their culture. Just like in the Book of Acts—the gypsies are seeing miracles on every hand, and the spread of the gospel not only in Romania, but to the gypsies in the neighboring countries as well. God showed me that when the Iron Curtain goes back up, He would use the gypsies to get the Word of God to places where no one else can go. Those people are going to be His evangelists when the times get rough. They can live on almost nothing and you can't keep them locked up; there's no Iron Curtain they can't get through!

What is this curse that is upon the gypsies? It is the curse of innocent blood. It is on them for betraying Jesus, the Son of God. The gypsies are in the bloodline of Judas Iscariot through his daughters.

THE CURSE OF INNOCENT BLOOD FOR BETRAYING THE SON OF GOD—JESUS

(Psalm 109:4-6) For my love they are my adversaries: but I give myself unto prayer.
And they have rewarded me evil for good, and hatred for my love.
Set thou a wicked man over him: and let Satan stand at his right hand.

INNOCENT BLOOD

What are these verses talking about? Judas was the trusted friend of Jesus and he turned away from his love. So what should have been blessings on the right hand were turned over to Satan.

(Psalm 109:7) When he shall be judged, let him be condemned:

Now in this verse is the start of the curse for betraying the Son of God. I think of it like in the old Wild West in America. We're going to have a trial and hang you. Remember the old western movies? Judas was judged to have done one of the most horrible deeds in all of history. His betrayal led to condemnation. That became a curse on all of the generations after him.

...and let his prayer become sin.

How would you like your prayers to become sin? This is the curse that the gypsies have carried through many generations! Just one of these things would be awful, but this curse just keeps on stacking up.

(Psalm 109:8-10) Let his days be few; and let another take his office.
Let his children be fatherless, and his wife a widow.

TURNING CURSES TO BLESSINGS

Let his children be continually vagabonds, and beg: let them seek their bread also out of their desolate places.

I have had experience with the gypsy people and have watched them and tried to minister to them. I have seen desperation in other cultures, but I have never seen desperation like gypsies have. I have never seen so many fatherless children.

Anywhere in the world where there is poverty, they will be there begging. If gypsies are born into the beggar class and have a girl (which in that culture is absolutely worthless), they'll do things like cut her tongue out, break her arms, and bind them up so they'll heal crooked. Then they set them up to beg so you'll feel sorry for them and give them money. I've seen this, folks; it's real today.

Gypsies often try to move into an area and set something up, but then they are driven away. The Public Broadcasting System had a TV program about them a while back and was pretty accurate about them, except in one thing. They said that there was no such thing as princes and kings with the gypsies. But there is such a thing. They have a beggar class that has to support their high class. These beggars have no excuse—"Well, I just had a hard day of begging and didn't get much." They have to turn over their money to their gypsy prince or king. They **have** to do this! It fits with what this verse is saying that much of their money goes to the extortioner.

INNOCENT BLOOD

(Psalm 109:12) Let there be none to extend mercy unto him: neither let there be any to favour his fatherless children.

I've never seen a people more cursed than the gypsies! Even in India, as bad as things are there, I don't see the curse on the people on the streets as bad as the one on the gypsies. Some gypsies have never even taken a bath. It's an amazing thing—dogs can discern gypsies. And everyone in Romania has dogs for that reason. A gypsy gets within half a block or so and dogs go crazy. Is not that something? We would hear them.

One time, when we were in Bucharest we finally got to bed after one or two in the morning, the dogs barked all night. They kept waking me up. I'd been two or three days without a full night's sleep. And I said, "Lord, I'm leaving. I'm going somewhere else. I can't go on without sleeping anymore. What is going on?" After a while you get tired enough that you accept rest, and I did. We kept asking ourselves why the dogs went crazy and we started watching. Every time the dogs went crazy, it was always because there were gypsies coming down the street.

(Psalm 109:13) Let his posterity be cut off; and in the generation following let their name be blotted out.

TURNING CURSES TO BLESSINGS

That means all the male bloodline—gone! The girls don't carry on the name of the father; they carry on the name of their husband, the male. But Judas' daughters had to go somewhere and get on with their lives. This is not just a generational curse, but also the curse of betraying the Lord Jesus Christ and of spilling innocent blood. This is the greatest depth of all the curses, the spilling of innocent blood.

(Psalm 109:14) Let the iniquity of his fathers be remembered with the LORD; and let not the sin of his mother be blotted out.

No forgiveness! This is the worst curse that anyone can get. And the worst thing was to betray the Lord Jesus Christ to death. This is prophecy about Judas Iscariot. If you don't believe it, read Acts 1:20. Jesus loves us when we don't deserve it. The last meal he had he shared with Judas. He tried to the last minute to win Judas and finally he said, "Whatever you do, do it quickly."

You should not think for one moment that there is anything in your life that could stop you from being able to get right into the throne room of God. You can expect deliverance from sin today, because it was bought by the blood of Jesus, by His death and resurrection. If Judas had repented, he would have been forgiven, too. And when the gypsies repent, the curse is broken in the name of Jesus.

INNOCENT BLOOD

(Psalm 109:15) Let them be before the LORD continually, that he may cut off the memory of them from the earth.

Everyone says, "Where did the gypsies come from anyway?" No one knows. There really is a gypsy kingdom; they do exist. They are people without a land, but with their own unique language. They know the gypsy language, but then learn every language wherever they go. The Iron Curtain was not able to keep them from moving. They move from nation to nation—we even have them in this nation. The gypsies are not a nation to be feared, but to be loved and respected and brought to the Lord Jesus, so they can be healed.

Curses, if they are not stopped, continue on. We have read about the kind of things that cause generational curses. Even the best families have them. The point is that despite the worst possible betrayal and committing of the murder of innocent blood, we, as well as the gypsies, can have complete deliverance. For Jesus became **"a curse for us: for it is written, Cursed is everyone that hangeth on a tree:" (Galatians 3:13).**

CURSES FROM ABORTION OF THE INNOCENT

Another very important issue that we have to face is the curse caused by the shedding of the innocent

TURNING CURSES TO BLESSINGS

blood of babies. Our whole nation has blood on its hands and is cursed by the lust for spilling innocent blood. We have something called abortion in this country. We need to repent for the shedding of innocent blood.

We've had about forty million babies killed in the womb, sacrificed to convenience. The way we get around this is that we have a debate about when life starts. You see, the issue is not about when life starts. The issue is that the little fetus has blood in it and is an innocent person. Abortion is murder and life is not in the breath only. My Bible says life is in the blood. You take a little fetus and take a razor to it and you'll see it bleed. It's a very serious thing. But, praise God, we're living in a time when we can have a personal relationship with God.

If anyone has had an abortion, we can have the curses broken in the name of Jesus and replaced with blessings. We have seen that curse removed and have seen the difference it makes in people's lives. But it's a serious thing that our nation faces, a very grave issue. Every twenty-two seconds there is an abortion done in the United States. Every minute and six seconds, three babies are sacrificed. The blood of all these babies is on the ground crying out to God! If you have had an abortion or been part of an abortion by recommending it or counseling someone to have one, please make sure you repent and get this curse broken.

INNOCENT BLOOD

I used to belong to a Christian denomination in which we believed that life was in the breath, so the baby was not alive until it squealed out at birth time. It's not right, folks. These are the kind of things that are destroying our nation. I had to repent of my sin of participating with abortion. I was sure glad to get rid of that curse. We prayed for several women who had had abortions who wanted to have children. They had tried all kinds of things for years, including the medical tests, and still couldn't have any children. Once the curse of innocent blood was broken in the name of Jesus and replaced with a blessing on the womb so they could bear children, God healed them completely and they now have beautiful little babies. God is so awesome!

CURSES FOR PREMEDITATED MURDER

Besides abortion, there are many other ways that people shed innocent blood. One is outright killing of an innocent man on purpose. One of King David's generals did that. I guess he thought he'd get in good with the boss by killing someone from the old regime.

(2 Samuel 3:28) And afterward when David heard it, he said, I and my kingdom are guiltless before the LORD for ever from the blood of Abner the son of Ner:

TURNING CURSES TO BLESSINGS

There was the spilling of innocent blood in this case, because Abner was a righteous man, a great man in Israel. That's why David would not accept what was done.

(2 Samuel 3:29) Let it rest on the head of Joab...

Joab supposedly went out to do David a favor, but he really did it because he thought it would be politically advantageous to him. David was not fooled by Joab's motives. So, he said, "Let it rest on Joab."

...and on all his father's house; and let there not fail from the house of Joab one that hath an issue, or that is a leper, or that leaneth on a staff, or that falleth on the sword, or that lacketh bread.

In other words, David made sure that that curse didn't land in his bloodline. Why did he do that? You might say, David didn't show much appreciation. But who was in David's bloodline? Jesus Christ was. Generational curses are real. David had to make sure he cleaned up his body and his life, or Jesus would not have accomplished His job.

Curses are a very serious thing. I'm not trying to make this heavy and I'm not trying to entertain you, either. I'm just laying down what the Lord wants us to see. We have things that we need to protect, and

INNOCENT BLOOD

innocent blood is the wrong thing to spill. If David had accepted what those men did, Jesus could not have set us free. God does not break rules. You know how you got rid of curses, under the law? There was not a guy whose name was Carl who came and ministered. They threw you in a hole and stoned you to death. It was not being stoned by heroin—it was with rocks!

Joab had done something that caused the curse of innocent blood. He had murdered someone innocent. And David sent it right back on Joab, because he would not take the responsibility for what Joab had done.

A few years ago in Bucharest, Romania, I was riding on the trolley and I heard this agonizing wailing sound that left me with a deep, lonely feeling. It passed, and I didn't think any more about it. A couple of days later, I was on a trolley in this same area and I heard the same sound. I started inquiring of the Lord and was waiting for an answer. That same afternoon, we passed that same spot again on the trolley and Emily, the interpreter, said to me, "That cemetery over there is for national heroes. The people buried there are the ones that were slaughtered during the revolution of 1989." I had my answer to what the sound was.

Then, I asked Emily, "Why do you call them innocent people?" She replied that during the revolution the citizens had no way to defend themselves. The oppressors had the guns, so they held hands in long chains of people and started marching across the countryside, singing praise and hymns to God. The military was ordered to shoot them and they did. But even the army didn't have the heart to continue to do what they were ordered. They refused to support the Communist dictator that had held Romania in poverty and oppression for so many years. This was the turning point to freedom for the country.

I anointed the gates of the cemetery with oil and prayed to break the curse of innocent blood in Jesus' name. I have been past that area dozens of times since, and have never heard innocent blood cry out again. God does hear innocent blood cry.

A record in the Bible that portrays this vividly is in Genesis 4.

(Genesis 4:8-11) And Cain talked with Abel his brother: and it came to pass, when they were in the field, that Cain rose up against Abel his brother, and slew him.

And the LORD said unto Cain, Where is Abel thy brother? And he said, I know not: Am I my brother's keeper?

And he said, What hast thou done? The voice of thy brother's blood crieth unto me from the ground.

And now art thou cursed from the earth, which hath opened her mouth to receive thy brother's blood from thy hand;

INNOCENT BLOOD

Cain will always be remembered and when someone does evil or if someone is a wild person, they say, they are out "raising Cain." The devastation of the spilling of the innocent blood of Abel literally was heard to be crying from the earth. God heard it and the curse followed.

If you or anyone you know of close to you has this curse, please repent and break the power of it in the name of Jesus. Healing **will** follow and lives will be restored.

Chapter 7
Known By Our Fruit

(Mark 11:12-14) And on the morrow, when they were come from Bethany, he was hungry:
And seeing a fig tree afar off having leaves, he came, if haply he might find any thing thereon: and when he came to it, he found nothing but leaves; for the time of figs was not yet.
And Jesus answered and said unto it, No man eat fruit of thee hereafter for ever. And his disciples heard it.

On the road to Bethany, Jesus talked to the fig tree and cursed it because it would bear no fruit. Jesus did this for a reason. He was not searching for figs at an off-season. If there was going to be fruit, there would have been sweet little buds or, as some people call them, fruit spurs. And there were none.

(Mark 11:20) And in the morning, as they passed by, they saw the fig tree dried up from the roots.

The fig tree dried from the bottom up, instead of from the top down.

(Mark 11:21) And Peter calling to remembrance saith unto him, Master,

TURNING CURSES TO BLESSINGS

behold, the fig tree which thou cursedst is withered away.

Do you know why Jesus cursed this fig tree? Because the fig tree was the symbol of Israel and it was not bearing fruit—something that was going on in Israel at that time. I've had people argue with me on his point, but I've talked to people who have studied and confirmed this truth. It makes a lot of sense. Why else would Jesus have done it? Just to show off the power of His words? He had already proven the power of His words. The reason he cursed it was because that tree was not producing and would not bear any fruit.

There is a curse on Israel today because they didn't bear fruit. They were all show to the other nations about how righteous they were; there were leaves, but no fruit. Israel as a nation denied the Lord Jesus Christ and didn't even recognize their Messiah when he came. There is so much grace that the Jewish people can now be forgiven, because they can be born again and set free from the curse that comes with the denial of Jesus.

This is where Christianity also is in so much trouble today. Many Christians either deny the Holy Spirit completely, or if they know about the Spirit, they emphasize being able to speak in tongues, interpret, discern, and do all nine gifts. And there's no fruit! The church at Corinth was puffed up and yet they were able to manifest all the spiritual gifts. They thought they were so right, yet they were practicing

KNOWN BY OUR FRUIT

incest. After all, "It's the grace administration, man, we can do as we please." Is it a true act of love for a man or woman to mess around with someone other than his or her own spouse? No! True love will bear fruit for all eternity.

Why would God permit people to continue to operate within His Spirit and still be full of sin? Do you know why? Because He's hoping to spare them, He's hoping that through it they will repent. But, guess what? Eventually, the day comes when the door closes. Some of us understand this. We've seen this happen to many ministries. Eventually the anointing of the Holy Spirit is removed. Then they have to go into all kinds of activity to try to make things work. The way a man or woman's ministry is known is by the fruit. It has nothing to do with anything else—the fruit tells all.

THE CURSE OF BEARING BAD FRUIT

Now let's talk about our life. What kind of fruit are we bearing? In these next verses, we're going to talk about rotten fruit. It's really interesting how God puts them both together. When we talk about the fruit of the flesh, the works of the flesh, we're talking about the side of us that does the bad. That's where we sin. That's the part where we deny God. It's the part where we get so bullheaded we're always in trouble.

TURNING CURSES TO BLESSINGS

(Galatians 5:19-21) Now the works of the flesh are manifest, which are these; Adultery, fornication, uncleanness, lasciviousness,

Idolatry, witchcraft, hatred, variance, emulations, wrath, strife, seditions, heresies,

Envyings, murders, drunkenness, revellings, and such like: of the which I tell you before, as I have also told you in time past, that they which do such things shall not inherit the kingdom of God.

Now that is rotten fruit! And those who practice those things do not have any inheritance in the kingdom of God. We just read it. I'll tell you, folks, it's the fruit that counts! You might have power and wealth, you may have all kinds of things working for you, you might have a fleet of jetliners taking your ministering teams everywhere, but these don't mean anything. It's the fruit that makes the difference. Israel is God's chosen nation and yet they became fruitless. Israel is God's chosen nation, and yet they killed the Son of God!

Rotten fruit! Have you ever heard, **"God is not mocked; what you sow, so shall you reap?"** The actions of Galatians 5:19-21 can literally rip your inheritance away. Some people believe it can cause you to go to hell, but I guarantee you that you lose your inheritance, because it says so. But let's not dwell on that. If that's what you are guilty of, then get the curses removed. This is what God wants us to be able to do, and this is what He rewards us for. We need to prune out the bad fruit.

This next verse, verse 22, is so much easier to read than the other one. This is the good fruit. This is what the Lord wants us to have: good fruit, not rotten fruit. He does not want His people to be caught up in envy and in murder and in drunkenness and in adultery. That's not God's will. That's the devil's will. Are those things forgivable? Yes, but what's the benefit of bad fruit? There is none.

THE GOOD FRUIT

(Galatians 5:22) But the fruit of the Spirit is love...

We've got to get love going, folks. You could be doing all kinds of things, but if your motivation is not love, and if your reason for doing things is anything but love, you're missing the boat. I'm not encouraging you to just give up because of lack of love, but to change your hearts and minds. Be love-driven. I want to be better. My hope and prayer is that I'll be better and that should be for every one of us.

Love is the first fruit mentioned because everything is built on love. It has to be love. Love is what you do, not how you feel. It is not how perfect we are. I'm a good example of that, of how God can use the foolish things of the world to confound the wise. It takes love. It takes love to do the will of God.

(John 3:16) For God so loved the world, that He gave His only-begotten Son, that whosoever believeth in him should not perish, but have everlasting life.

Jesus so loved the world. He so loved you that He became a curse for you. You never achieve love to the point that you can say, "Been there, done that." It does not work like that. Love is something you have to keep working on because it is the number one fruit.

The reason I understand love is number one is that it is the first one mentioned in the list. But God also taught me this principle in a vision. You see, if you don't walk in love, you might have a lot of charisma, but you have problems with your fruit. The first one is love! The vision was of a pipe with the water running out into nine 5-gallon paint buckets. The water started running into the first bucket, which is love, and then overflowed into the second, which is joy. This went all down the line. The water wouldn't run into the next one until the first bucket was full. You don't get this fruit all in a cluster. Until love overflows, we can't have joy. You can't keep the love in the bucket; it has to overflow before you can fill the joy bucket.

KNOWN BY OUR FRUIT

...joy,

Joy is important because the joy of the Lord is your strength. But the enemy would like to steal your joy, if he can, so he can weaken you. Otherwise, he can't beat you. Look, if the joy of the Lord is your strength, Satan has to steal your strength, your joy, in order to be successful against you. But when your joy is full, he can't even get into the same room with you! Joy is really important, but when the joy is lacking, walking in love is how we fill the joy bucket.

...peace,

Until love and joy overflow, there can't be peace. "Unity in the Spirit in the bond of peace" is not about doctrine. God didn't put these fruit in this order by accident. I've had to change so many doctrines that I held before. And I thought I had it down pat. I still think I've got it down pat, and then the Lord shows me how my doctrine needs some fine-tuning and I have to change again! God gives more grace to the humble. Our humility does not have to be to people, but it has to be to God. The word "Lord" means, "Boss." So, when he says that we should do something, we don't go by how we feel but we take him at his word. By the way, it is love to obey. That results in joy and then yields a peace in your heart. The joy bucket cascades into the peace bucket!

TURNING CURSES TO BLESSINGS

...longsuffering,

You can't have longsuffering unless love, joy, and peace are already there. Otherwise, you would just be worshipping your suffering. Then you'd have a suffering ceremony and invite people over. You'd publish suffering newsletters and you'd say, "Look at my scars!"

...gentleness,

I'll tell you, it took a lot of love for me to become gentle, because I was not gentle. You really have to work on these things. I'm a warrior and I admit that I love to fight and I love to get into battle. But if you get so caught up in the battle all the time, you're not gentle when you need to be. So, what brings a balance? Love, joy, peace, and longsuffering! These have to overflow before there can be gentleness.

...goodness

Goodness is the next bucket in line. All of this fruit is not something you accomplish and polish up and put a wax coat on it. You're supposed to feed on it. This fruit is Spirit food! You've heard of soul food? Well, this is Spirit food. There really is a difference between soul and spirit. By the way, I do like soul food, but I love Spirit food more! This fruit is fruit of the Spirit. You get weary and then you grab one of those big old goodness fruits and you eat. Do you notice how you like to have an apple shine, even if you do eat it? This fruit is there to feed on and God help you if there is no fruit in your basket!

Do you see why Israel became so miserable? They got to the point, where there was no fruit in their basket, and they denied the Lord Jesus. We as Christians have to be very careful that we do not fall into the same trap.

...faith,

Once you have the rest of the fruit, you will have faith. You can even have a faith ministry. This is easy to achieve because you have all this fruit just pushing right along. And how does faith come? We are used to hearing that 'faith comes by hearing, and hearing by the word of God." Faith also comes as we walk in the other fruit, starting with love.

Faith is spiritual. Many times new Christians or weakened Christians try to make themselves faith Christians. But this is something that you cannot do on your own. Becoming a faith Christian requires doing the love and filling the preceding buckets. Your faith will build and overflow because all of this is pointing to a relationship with the Lord Jesus. As we walk in love, we walk with Jesus.

...meekness,

Until faith and all the fruit preceding it overflows, we can't have meekness. Being meek is saying, O.K.,

TURNING CURSES TO BLESSINGS

Lord, I'll do it! Can I choose where, how and when I'm going to be meek? No! God wants meekness from us. We can get to the point where we are so caught up in our own game plan, that it can become a god to us. We have to be very careful that we are meek according to God's word.

...temperance: against such there is no law.

This "such" includes all the fruit, not just temperance. There are people who want to say, "I don't live under the law; this is the grace administration and I can do what I please. I know about dispensations." This is the grace administration, but we cannot live under the fullness of grace unless we have fruit of the Spirit in our lives. If we live in sin, it brings rotten flesh fruit. Doing things by the flesh brings us under the Law. The Law is for the lawless. The kind of fruit we have in our life or the lack of good fruit shows how much authority the Law still has.

If we are lacking good fruit in our life, we need to go back to the love bucket and make sure it does not have a hole in it. Fill up your buckets, starting with love and watch how they overflow to produce much spiritual fruit. The fresh overflowing will always be evident.

Chapter 8
Cursed by Disobedience

Naaman was the captain of the host of Syria and a mighty man of valor, but he had leprosy. He had come to Elisha, the man of God to be healed and Elisha had told him to go dip in the Jordan seven times to be healed from his leprosy. At first Naaman didn't like the idea of getting into a filthy river, but when he finally did it, he was healed. He had wanted to reward the man of God for having healed the leprosy, but the prophet sent him on his way. His servant Gehazi decided that he knew better than Elisha and disobeyed. The result was that he was cursed.

(2 Kings 5:26-27) And he said unto him, Went not mine heart with thee, when the man turned again from his chariot to meet thee? Is it a time to receive money, and to receive garments, and oliveyards, and vineyards, and sheep, and oxen, and menservants, and maidservants?
The leprosy therefore of Naaman shall cleave unto thee, and unto thy seed for ever." And he went out from his presence a leper as white as snow.

TURNING CURSES TO BLESSINGS

Gehazi had disobeyed the man of God, which was like disobeying God. He got the same leprosy that Naaman had been delivered from. When we don't do the will of the Lord, it always brings curses, as we have seen previously.

THE DEVIL IS CURSED

God cursed the devil, that wily serpent, for his disobedience in the Garden.

(Genesis 3:14) And the LORD God said unto the serpent, Because thou hast done this, thou art cursed above all cattle, and above every beast of the field; upon thy belly shalt thou go, and dust shalt thou eat all the days of thy life:

God told the devil back in Genesis and it's still true today, **"And dust shall thou eat all the days of thy life."** You have the authority in Christ to bruise the devil's head. He's crawling on his belly. You don't even have to jump up to bruise his head and to cave it in! He's on his belly; he's in the dust. Listen, if he starts causing you grief and if you'll stand on the Word, guess what? You can fill him up with dust! Why do you think Jesus said to his disciples when He was sending them out, "If they reject you, shake the dust off your feet"? It was a symbol; it was a curse that went on that village.

CURSED BY DISOBEDIENCE

Do you know what has happened in Christianity? We have elevated the devil by making such commonly heard statements as, "Boy, the devil sure has me under attack," and "The adversary really got to me this time." By making such statements, the devil is able to say, "Yes, give me some more praise! Give me some more praise!" If you are guilty of this, repent and know, **"...greater is he that is in you, than he that is in the world" (1 John 4:4).**

We have missed this one. Jesus didn't miss anything. Jesus defeated the devil. We are permitting him to get a hold of our children, and to get a hold of our nation. The only power he has is what he has stolen from us. Jesus said in John 10:10: **"The thief cometh not, but for to steal, and to kill, and to destroy: I am come that they might have life, and that they might have it more abundantly."**

The prophecy about Jesus is in Genesis 3 and God said it straight from the beginning:

(Genesis 3:15) And I will put enmity between thee and the woman, and between thy seed and her seed; it shall bruise thy head, and thou shalt bruise his heel.

We have the authority to bruise the devil's head, to cave it right in! Have you ever been bruised in the head? I have had a few shiners in my day. I know what having a bruised head is all about. If you get hit in the head, you can't stay on your feet. The authority we have, because of Jesus, is a blast to the head of the devil. It's time to take back our ground!

(John 14:12) Verily, verily, I say unto you, He that believeth on me, the works that I do shall he do also; and greater works than these shall he do…"

If it is going to be a battle, which one is worse---a bruise on the head or one on the heel? In the battle, you have got the edge. You have a promise from God. It's **"Christ in you, the hope of glory."** You are God's child if you have Christ in you. This is about taking a stand and putting the devil in his place, which is down in the dust. This is one curse that we don't need to break. The devil is going to get the results of all his deceit!

CURSES FROM RELATIVES

Have you ever been cursed by a relative? Every one of us has. Grandma Eve and Grandpa Adam are in our bloodline. God cursed all of us when He cursed Adam and Eve because of their disobedience.

From Grandma Eve

(Genesis 3:16) Unto the woman he said, I will greatly multiply thy sorrow and thy conception; in sorrow thou shalt bring forth

CURSED BY DISOBEDIENCE

children; and thy desire shall be to thy husband, and he shall rule over thee.

God told the woman that her sorrow and also her conception would be multiplied. Childbearing is a difficult time as any woman who has had a child can tell you. There is a curse on the woman and she will have pain in childbirth. Also, in this day and time, there is PMS (pre-menstrual syndrome) that is a part of the curse that came with the original fall. Women tell me that it is worse today. Maybe it is because today there is more evil, or it might be from all the innocent blood being spilled.

From Grandpa Adam

(Genesis 3:17) And unto Adam he said, Because thou hast hearkened unto the voice of thy wife, and hast eaten of the tree, of which I commanded thee, saying, Thou shalt not eat of it: cursed is the ground for thy sake; in sorrow shalt thou eat of it all the days of thy life;

Men don't need to feel left out. They have been cursed also. This is really important. You need to listen to God, even if your wife gets mad at you. If you make your decisions according to what the Word says, she'll come around. If you give in and do her

TURNING CURSES TO BLESSINGS

will, you will have trouble. Our labor and sorrow now are the result of what he did then.

(Genesis 3:18-19) Thorns also and thistles shall it bring forth to thee; and thou shalt eat the herb of the field;
In the sweat of thy face shalt thou eat bread, till thou return unto the ground; for out of it wast thou taken: for dust thou art, and unto dust shalt thou return.

This is the curse that we received from Grandpa Adam. Man's work was very hard after God cursed Adam. This one is easy to see every time we work hard and the sweat comes down our brow. I've been told that going against God is not a serious thing, but here we are still suffering today from that curse. We have to go through this work if we want to get paid so we can take care of our family. Have you ever heard of somebody being paid for not going to work?

Some days I have come home from work so tired that I can't even enjoy my supper. My wife is thinking, "He does not even appreciate that I've worked so hard on this meal." It was because that day was so tough. Tough days like this are the result of Adam's disobedience against God, which is a very serious matter. The price of disobedience is devastating, not only for us, but for our children. And it will only get worse, if we do not repent.

CURSED BY DISOBEDIENCE

CURSES FROM IDOLATRY

There is only one God. But if you want to make enemies, just take away someone's idols. People kill over that. My ancestors came from Ireland and the English decided they wanted to dominate the Emerald Isles, so they used religion. Today these same people kill, on both sides, over Jesus—the orange and the green. It goes on all over the world. Just go to Bosnia or Kosovo and you will see a thousand-year-old war over idolatry.

Genesis 31 has a record about a curse that happened because of stealing someone's idols. Jacob and Rachel had left her father's house and were on their way back to Canaan. To be able to have Rachel, the one promised to him, Jacob had had to work an extra seven years. His father-in-law, Laban, had required Jacob to work for him for fourteen years in order to marry his daughters. But when Jacob and his family sneaked off in the middle of the night, Rachel took some of her father's gods.

(Genesis 31:30, 31) And now, though thou wouldest needs be gone, because thou sore longedst after thy father's house, yet wherefore hast thou stolen my gods?
And Jacob answered and said to Laban, Because I was afraid: for I said, Peradventure thou wouldest take by force thy daughters from me.

TURNING CURSES TO BLESSINGS

Laban was not a nice father-in-law. Jacob was afraid he wanted to steal his daughters back, the wives for whom he had worked so hard.

(Genesis 31:32) With whomsoever thou findest thy gods, let him not live: before our brethren discern thou what is thine with me, and take it to thee. For Jacob knew not that Rachel had stolen them.

Here is where Jacob cursed his wife unknowingly. It is easy to say things, but you can't put that bullet back in the gun once you've squeezed the trigger. The bullet has a primer that gives it the spark, which explodes the gunpowder. You can't ever take it back. Think about that when you speak words.

Here's how this principle hurt Jacob. He lost his wife as a result of his words. Jacob cursed Rachel to death. He cursed his precious wife. When Rachel left, she stole her father's favorite graven images. And, of course, he came for them because they were his favorites. He didn't come to ask Jacob, "Why did you leave?" He said, "You took my gods!"

(Genesis 31:33) And Laban went into Jacob's tent, and into Leah's tent, and into the two maidservants' tents; but he found them not. Then went he out of Leah's tent, and entered into Rachel's tent.

CURSED BY DISOBEDIENCE

Laban first went to the tent of those he suspected the most, then to the next and the next. He did not go to his favorite daughter's tent until last. She was his pet and he never thought she would do such a thing.

(Genesis 31:34) Now Rachel had taken the images, and put them in the camel's furniture, and sat upon them. And Laban searched all the tent, but found them not.

The camel's furniture was not a couch and a coffee table. It was a frame that went over the camel to carry loads. It was a bulky frame and they stored it in the tent.

(Genesis 31:35) And she said to her father, Let it not displease my lord that I cannot rise up before thee; for the custom of women is upon me. And he searched, but found not the images.

Rachael acted as if she revered her father, but nice words don't always mean a nice heart. Did she really think of him as her lord if she did such a thing to him? She told him she was having her menstrual cycle, but that may not have been so. It could have been a lie.

According to the customs of the time, the menstrual cycle was cause for a woman to be considered unclean. Men were to stay away from her. Rachael told her father that, knowing he would respect her and not insist on the search. She thought she had so cleverly deceived her father, because he did not find the idols hidden under her seat. She thought she had deceived everyone, but let's see what the Word of God says.

(Genesis 31:36) And Jacob was wroth, and chided with Laban: and Jacob answered and said to Laban, What is my trespass? what is my sin, that thou hast so hotly pursued after me?

Now, it is proven that Laban was wrong because he could not find the idols. Jacob gets very brave. If he had had the nerve to stand up to the man from the very beginning, none of this would have happened. And because of fear, he cursed his wife to death. Rachel only lived four more chapters in the book of Genesis.

(Genesis 35:16-19) And they journeyed from Bethel; and there was but a little way to come to Ephrath: and Rachel travailed, and she had hard labour.
And it came to pass, when she was in hard labour, that the midwife said unto her, Fear not; thou shalt have this son also.

CURSED BY DISOBEDIENCE

And it came to pass, as her soul was in departing, (for she died) that she called his name Ben-oni: but his father called him Benjamin.
And Rachel died, and was buried in the way to Ephrath, which is Beth-lehem.

Rachael died as a result of Jacob saying, "Whoever has stolen your gods, let him die!" The curse truly came to pass. You have to be very careful because you can curse someone you dearly love. Whenever you're going to say hateful things, bite your tongue. Don't make statements out of fear. In James 3:10, it says: **"Out of the same mouth proceedeth blessing and cursing."** We have the privilege of choosing which we will speak. It also says in the Bible that we will be judged for every idle word we say. We will not get by with these things. Praise God for the option of repentance!

Chapter 9
What Is In Your Home?

I was in the home of a very wealthy and respected gypsy man, a member of the Romanian parliament. I was in the back room praying with the mother, father, and grandmother of a five year-old child. For two and a half years, the granddaughter had been crying and whimpering nonstop. They had taken her to the best specialists all over Europe and no one could figure out what was the matter with her. The grandparents, who had been to the church services where I was teaching, had begged me to come and pray for their little granddaughter. I had gone with them and started praying for the girl. I also prayed for an elderly woman who had been tortured in a Communist prison for fourteen years for being a Christian. The only thing that she needed to have done to get out of prison was to say that Jesus was dead. She refused to do that.

We were ministering to the little girl and broke the curse that was on her in the name of Jesus. We put blessings in its place and she started smiling and laughing and flirting with her grandmother. Then all of a sudden we heard a commotion in the living room where most of the people were gathered. In the corner of the living room had been a table that was now scattered in very small pieces all over the floor. Everyone was in shock!

The table had held an object that was a gift to the grandfather. When we removed the curse from the

TURNING CURSES TO BLESSINGS

little girl, the object had exploded and was destroyed. The object had been cursed and had been the source of the curse for the little girl.

The people in the room were astounded when they saw the girl smiling and laughing and not crying at all. One of the men in the living room came up and begged me to help him. He confessed that he was a false Christian, an infiltrator. He would go to church and hang around with all the believers, saying he was one also. The man confessed his betrayal, asked God to forgive his sins and to give him new life. Then he requested to be baptized, so we baptized him in the only place around, the bathtub!

Neither the grandparents of the little girl, nor the other gypsies present that night, would have ever thought that beautiful object on the table in the corner was cursed. It is so easy to be deceived! Only God can show us the truth. The grandmother was so delighted that she said, "If there is anything in this house that is cursed, blow it up! Even blow up my house, if necessary. I love God and my family."

When my wife and I moved from Albuquerque, New Mexico, to western Tennessee, we noticed something so different for us. While Albuquerque is in the high desert, western Tennessee is part of the Mississippi valley area where everything is very green. We thought it was great the way everyone mowed their lawns—I mean, everyone! The lawns are very large and very well kept, no matter how small and humble the houses. When I started having to mow

WHAT IS IN YOUR HOME?

our lawn, at first I was so busy that I would let the grass get a little high. I'm talking about maybe four or five inches high. I thought it still looked pretty. Well, I learned very fast why you should keep your lawn mowed short! Snakes hide in the grass! I didn't have any idea that there are poisonous snakes all over the area and lawn mowing is a safety measure.

That is the way things are with witchcraft and sorcery. Things can look pretty good on the surface, but hiding inside is a poisonous curse.

PROFESSIONAL CURSES (WITCHCRAFT)

As I mentioned at the beginning of the book, professional curses are very common in many countries around the world. There are curses that a person pays for to put on someone else, or that another pays to put upon us. Most of the time you don't even know that you have been cursed. It is like walking through the grass and finding a poisonous snake in the middle of that beautiful green pasture. It's easy to be unaware of them.

The following are only a few examples of what witches use to curse people. The list is endless and many books have been written about this particular aspect of curses. In fact, witchcraft is usually the first thing people think of when I mention anything about curses. Most people don't even realize that it's only a very small part of the whole subject. Praise God, that He's given us so much in His Word to help us understand the strategies of Satan to keep people from knowing God. Whenever we do things that stop others from getting close to the Lord, we might as well say it is witchcraft. Call it what it really is!

I have even heard of pastors and their wives saying it is all right to use white magic. Anyone who tries to use spiritual power without God—I don't care how good it is—is still using witchcraft. Do you know what happened to people in the Old Testament who practiced these things? They were killed! Check it out in Exodus 22:18.

One of the methods professionals use to curse others is to put curses on objects, and then get them into the homes of the people they are trying to curse. We cannot do anything about an object that has been dedicated to Satan and darkness to make it clean. It has have been consecrated to evil. But we can sure destroy it, keep away from it, and reject it.

CURSED OBJECTS

I am telling you about these things because it can happen to anyone, anywhere in the world. It does not just happen to gypsies in Romania! There are many things being taken into the homes of Christians that have been cursed by professional witches or sorcerers. These can be gifts. Or they can be objects hidden, or buried in the yard by someone else. They are also things that we buy. We think we bought something "so beautiful." Yet we have just cursed ourselves by

WHAT IS IN YOUR HOME?

bringing a cursed object into our home. This is harder to recognize when someone gives us a cursed thing as a special present, like what happened in the case of the gypsy family. I even know Christian parents who have a hard time getting rid of cursed objects that "new age" teachers at school had their children make in art classes. Here in the United States, it is common, for example, for children to make Indian "dream catchers" in school. Parents have to educate their children about these things!

When it comes to professional curses, we have to really watch out. If we are obedient to the Lord our God, He will help us and protect us. He will make sure that we receive notice about something that was imposed on us, or that we imposed on ourselves. God is not in the business of death! He does not want us to get cut off because of a curse that someone paid to put on us. This means that we must be straight with God—single-minded—and when we say we're going to get rid of something, we do it.

A couple, which is very close to me, found out that could not play around with cursed objects. They live and work in Washington State, and spend a lot of time doing technical work like charting the bottom of the ocean for making navigational maps. They had been visiting us in New Mexico. The husband, who loves Indian things, was intrigued with the Kachina dolls made by the Indians of New Mexico. I told them to leave the Kachina dolls alone because they are cursed objects. The Indians who make them laugh

TURNING CURSES TO BLESSINGS

at all the tourists that buy this type of object. The tourists have no idea what curses they are taking with them.

When the couple left us in their nice four-wheel-drive Nissan, they decided to go through an area where there are some Indian ruins, the Chaco Canyon. These are some of the most important Indian ruins on the North American continent. Thousands of people had to have lived there at one time. As they drove through, a gust of wind came up and rolled their car over, destroying it. They were on a dirt road in the late afternoon. It was not tourist season, so there was no one around. But a man saw them from his car a few miles away. When he got into Farmington, New Mexico, he called the highway patrol.

When the patrol arrived to rescue them they found that these folks had had to build a fire to keep warm because they couldn't take shelter in their crushed car. They had been there waiting for help for four or five hours. As if they hadn't had enough trouble already, the first thing the policeman did when he arrived was to write them a ticket for careless driving. He added anything else he could think of to make up a $600 dollar fine. He was not even concerned whether they were alive or dead.

They called me up and when I got there I said, "I don't want any Kachina dolls in my pickup." The man said, "What makes you think we have any?" But his wife just squirmed and said, "You can't fool Carl." We

WHAT IS IN YOUR HOME?

went through everything until we found the doll. I stomped on it, totally destroying it. Even the man in the junkyard kept saying, "I'll take it!" But there was no way I was going to curse him.

How about Buddhas? Some people have a little Buddha in their home. They say, "But he's so cute, with his fat little belly!" He is not. He is a false god. How about other kinds of ancient objects? People think it is so wonderful to have antique things, especially from archeological digs. I could tell story after story of curses I have had to break from people who have picked these things up. There are many objects of this kind that come in and destroy.

For instance, do you know what the New Agers are doing? (By the way, New Agers are not really new. They come from Nimrod, of ancient Babylonia!) They are putting spells on things they make themselves, saying they are made by ancient people. People buy them, too. We were in a home once in which the children played with "dream catchers." Most of the New Age things that are in round shapes are channels for demons, such as wreaths, leis (flowered necklace wreaths) from Hawaii, and some kinds of necklaces.

Tarot cards, Ouija boards, crystals, and dream-catchers are only a few of these kinds of objects. The Indians make the dream-catchers to weave spells with. "Oh, but they are just funny little things!" No, they are not! If you are asking information from a crystal ball, whether it be in the form of a pendant or something you hold in your hand, get rid of it! You're

TURNING CURSES TO BLESSINGS

supposed to be going to God for information! Those objects are evil and are meant for evil. If you have them, get rid of them! At least, that's what I would do in my house.

Many times our children bring cursed objects into our homes. For instance, if something "natural" has anyone mesmerized by its beauty, it could very well be cursed. Once my granddaughter found a beautiful black feather that was so black, it shone blue. She brought it into the house with my daughter's permission. Soon everything started going wrong. Every word they spoke in the privacy of their home was repeated back to them by people outside their family who had not been there at the time. When the object was removed, all the bad things stopped happening. But also God opened the doors of heaven. They started getting back many times over what was taken from them.

Children bring toys into the house that we don't even think about. I recommend that you ask God whether any items in the house are cursed, starting with your children's toys. Get all these items out of your house. If you're not sure about whether something is cursed or not, I'd get rid of it!

Another thing that is dangerous is a wreath, any wreath. Wreaths are considered portals for evil spirits to come in. I know of a lady who had a beautiful flower arrangement in the shape of a wreath over her bedroom door. It was cursed because of the type of dried flowers used in it and it was the gateway for the

WHAT IS IN YOUR HOME?

devil to get in to cause division in her household. The Hawaiian leis are along the same line, letting the spirits come in. The leis are placed on couples as they arrive in Hawaii. They are part of a fertility goddess rite. These things are consecrated for evil and they cannot be made good!

Use wisdom regarding video games. If you have brought something like this into your house and you have noticed a change in behavior in anyone who lives there, back track and see what it was. Your children can bring evil things into the house and you don't even realize it. Smash those video games. They are stealing your children. The boys who did the shootings in Colorado, in the Columbine High School, were playing these games. We all saw and heard the results of their "entertainment!"

Did you know that many cartoon series shown on television teach young children to accept curses on themselves? I've also seen on Christian television things like Virtual-Reality Theater that are just as evil. Why settle for virtual reality, when God will give His people dreams and visions of the truth? Have you ever seen a vision? Talk about detail! God's Word says that in the end times we will have visions. The Romanian Christians say that Americans have television—so there's no vision. But you should see all the godly visions the Romanian Christians have. They are truly amazing.

Another category of objects to be aware of is religious objects. Some of the things people consider

TURNING CURSES TO BLESSINGS

sacred are really cursed because of idolatry. As far as I'm concerned, these things aren't Christian. These include icons, statues, and crosses that have Jesus still hanging on them. If Jesus is still on the cross, then he is not resurrected. How do you think that God feels when he looks down on a Christian's neck and sees his Son like that, after all he went through?

I know a man who has the grim reaper tattooed on his body (the spirit of death with a sickle in his hand). There is already suicide in past generations of his family, so all that tattoo does for him is just give him a self-imposed death curse. Tattoos are very evil, because they can't be taken off. Just that in itself is a curse. And God speaks against painting or tattooing our bodies.

There are people who paint hex signs on their barns thinking they are taking off evil. But they are actually cursing themselves. You may say I'm crazy, but not about this! I've seen what happens.

Many churches have a sign in stained glass, the wheel of eternity, of evolution, and you wonder why churches are falling apart. An art movement, very popular in religious circles, is the renaissance movement with its paintings, sculptures, and murals. These are the icons, or pictures, which show the nice glow behind Jesus' head. Do you think Jesus walked on this earth with a glow behind his head? No, He walked like you and me. He stubbed his toes, cracked his knuckles, hurt his thumbnail helping his father to build furniture. And in all these things, He never said

WHAT IS IN YOUR HOME?

a bad word. These icons are being used by witches to promote evil.

CURSED PLACES

If things start going wrong at home and you don't have any cursed objects there, check your house. Maybe the people who lived in it before had some kind of problem.

I had to pray one time with a couple that was having problems in a house they had just moved into. First, they had problems with their little son. He hated being in his room and couldn't sleep at night. Dreams terrorized him, about homosexuals doing something to him. After that, they moved the child out and set up the father's office there. Guess what? He couldn't work in there, either! His head would start spinning around and he found it difficult to concentrate.

When they called me for prayer, we walked all through the house praying. Although they didn't know it when they moved in, the people who had lived there before were homosexuals. I asked them if they had noticed anything unusual in the house when they bought it. The wife said that she noticed there were some signs painted on the wall of the closet where the little boy was to sleep. But she painted over them and figured it was all right. I explained to them that those were special symbols that were cursing the house. Just painting over them does not get rid of the curse.

TURNING CURSES TO BLESSINGS

The parents did not believe that it was necessary to remove the whole wall of the closet to get rid of the curse. But that very night, the boy had the worst nightmare of all. The next morning the mother went into the closet with a hammer and tore out the whole wall. God honored her act to look after her son. That same afternoon, a contractor just happened to stop by with extra materials from a job and built a brand new wall in the closet for free. After that, the little boy didn't have any more of those nightmares.

CURSED ANIMALS

People involved in occult practices like witchcraft and sorcery use animals for many different evil purposes. They can put curses on people through them. For example, we have things like the Easter bunny and Easter eggs. These are idolatrous objects. Since times of antiquity, bunnies and eggs were used in the worship of the goddess of fertility and springtime. The goddess' name is Astarte or Ishtar (later forms were Oestre, becoming our modern word "Easter"). She is as old as the Babylonian and Egyptian demons. I don't get too upset about people celebrating Easter, as long as they don't worship those objects. In fact, I'm glad that at least once a year people recognize that Jesus died and rose again! It's interesting that this goddess is worshipped in the Middle East and in the United States, but there is no such thing in Latin America. There they have another

WHAT IS IN YOUR HOME?

goddess instead. Each area of the world has specific animals that are either worshipped or are part of their rites.

The devil is trying to bring us down. We **can** save our homes; we **can** save our nation. There is something we can do about it. **You** can save your marriage and your children. If you have a healthy home, keep it that way and help other people to have healthy homes. Clearing our homes of cursed objects is one of the best places to begin!

Always check your house to see what's left behind when other people come into your house, even for a visit. In war, you would always check these things. If you are spending time with people who are not causing you to stand strong, confront them. Start talking about Jesus. That will send them away if they do not want to change. If you have relationships and friendships that lead you away from Jesus Christ, the only one that will get you to God is the relationship with Jesus Christ. Whenever you do things that stop you from getting close to the Lord, you open the doors for devastating curses in your life.

In order to be set free from the results of cursed objects and these types of curses, there is a very important action that is required. Turn yourself over to Jesus Christ. Make Jesus the Lord of your life, not yourself. Making a little confession down on your knees is not something you do once in your life, or even once a week. You have to do this every day. You may be tempted to do wrong instead of doing what is

TURNING CURSES TO BLESSINGS

right, but you make a decision to do what is right. Why? Because Jesus is Lord. He is our Boss.

This is very important. Cleaning out our homes of curses objects (which permit the devil to impact our lives) is a necessary part of being able to live lives that are dedicated to Christ. Clean up your home and it will be a blessing to all who live there and to all who visit. We must become aware of how the enemy infiltrates and sneaks in to try to ruin our close, day-by-day relationship with the Lord.

Chapter 10
Self-imposed Curses

A curse cannot land without a cause, neither is it always brought on us by other people, intentionally or unintentionally. The truth of the matter is that we like to shoot ourselves in the foot! We tend to curse ourselves right and left. Is not that strange? It is time we understood how serious this matter is!

Many times, by our words, we end up imposing generational curses on ourselves. Let me explain. Suppose there is a curse from past generations in your family, handed down from parent to child. The curse is: "All Simpson males are failures!" If you're a male in Bart Simpson's family, this can make you feel that you are so doomed to failure. You get desperate. You say, "I'm not going to succeed." Guess what you're doing? You have taken an inherited curse and nailed it down on yourself. You have imposed a curse on yourself. The generational curse is made stronger by being self-imposed as well.

The following account in the Bible is incredible because there are so many curses tied into one to another. We read part of it before in the chapter on "Does God Curse?"

(Genesis 27:11-12) And Jacob said to Rebekah his mother, Behold, Esau my brother is a hairy man, and I am a smooth man:

TURNING CURSES TO BLESSINGS

My father peradventure will feel me, and I shall seem to him as a deceiver; and I shall bring a curse upon me, and not a blessing.

When Jacob's mother was endeavoring to get him to steal the blessing from Esau, this was Jacob's response. The younger son knew all about curses. He was well aware that there is a curse that comes upon you if you cause the blind to wander, if you deceive a blind or handicapped person. Isaac was blind by this time and could not see which son was which. Curses bring so many other curses. That is why they have such intense results. This chapter of Genesis illustrates many kinds of curses. The following verse shows how words can impose a curse on ourselves.

(Genesis 27:13) And his mother said unto him, Upon me be thy curse, my son: only obey my voice, and go fetch me them.

Rebekah imposed that curse on herself. What was she thinking, anyway? She just condemned herself to death!

How do we impose curses on ourselves? If you have alcoholism in your family and you start drinking, you have self-imposed the alcoholism. Now you are not only dealing with a generational curse, but you have given that curse twice as much authority in your life. I lived a wild life and I was nearly thirty before I came back to the Lord. I imposed a lot of curses on

SELF IMPOSED CURSES

myself and I had to ask God to forgive me so I could break all of those curses. One of the excuses I had for being such a hellion was that "I'm not going to live much past forty, so I'm going to pack in a hundred years of living!" I was actually imposing a death curse on myself by confessing the generational curse that all the male Foxes died young from heart failure. I would probably have died at that age. Since the curses were removed, the Lord has blessed me. I have already outlived most of the males in my family by many years. I've spent these years living for Him.

I know a girl in whose family all the women had died of breast cancer. So, when she got a small cyst that the doctor said was benign, she went ahead and had him cut off both breasts just to keep from getting breast cancer. The doctor went along with it. This young mother had this done to her and guess what? Two years later, she got breast cancer! You cannot surgically remove curses. They are spiritually caused and they have to be dealt with spiritually. I'm not saying whether or not you should have surgery. That's not the issue. This young woman had the curses broken and replaced with blessings and was totally healed of the cancer. Then she made sure the curses were broken off her three little girls and replaced with blessings.

Just because a doctor tells you something does not mean it's true. If you accept a diagnosis that is false, you may be imposing a curse upon yourself. My greatest fantasy is going into a hospital and praying for everybody and they will all walk out healed. I am going to hang on to that fantasy. I want to do that! Many times, the staff of a hospital has not wanted me to go in to pray for people. But sometimes you have to go do what it takes to get the job done! We don't have to be dependent on things outside of God. We have the authority to change things, if we choose. Check everything you are told, even by a "professional," before you accept it as true.

THE GENERATIONAL SELF IMPOSED CURSE OF THE JEWS

Why did the Jews suffer in the Holocaust? They brought it upon themselves. I am not against Jewish people, but they brought the curse of innocent blood upon themselves by begging Pilate to crucify Jesus. Pilate had wanted to let Jesus go, and the people would not allow it.

(Matthew 27:24, 25) When Pilate saw that he could prevail nothing, but that rather a tumult was made, he took water, and washed his hands before the multitude, saying, I am innocent of the blood of this just person: see ye to it.
Then answered all the people, and said, His blood be on us, and on our children.

SELF IMPOSED CURSES

All the people answered this, not just the leadership. I had a Jewish man try to tell me, "I don't have this curse on me because it was said only for the leaders, the elders." So, I said to him: "Read your Bible. What does it say?" It says, "All the people said."

The curse was imposed for how many generations? There is no end stated there. Jews have the same chance that we Gentiles do. Jesus is their salvation, too. This is a self-imposed curse of innocent blood that became a generational curse. People ask why the Jews suffered so much in Germany. If they had said something different back in Jesus' time, history would have been different for them. Words make a big difference. World War II is not the only time that the Jews have suffered persecution. It has become part of the record of their history.

CURSES A NATION IMPOSES ON ITSELF

(Deuteronomy 19:10-12) That innocent blood be not shed in thy land, which the LORD thy God giveth thee for an inheritance, and so blood be upon thee.

But if any man hate his neighbour, and lie in wait for him, and rise up against him, and smite him mortally that he die, and fleeth into one of these cities:

Then the elders of his city shall send and fetch him thence, and deliver him into

TURNING CURSES TO BLESSINGS

the hand of the avenger of blood, that he may die.

Our nation is cursed because we are protecting the criminal. The cities of refuge did not protect cold-blooded murderers. A curse that is on our nation that we need to repent of is that victims, not criminals, are persecuted, prosecuted, and destroyed. The rapists, murderers, thieves, and drug dealers run free. Those people dealing drugs are dealing death. If you have family members that are dealing death, pray for them. Do not make excuses for them. Not only could they burn in hell, so could the people that are making money from them.

If the elders had not released the man that had shed innocent blood, even though he fled to the city of refuge, they would have been damned. The elders of the city would have brought damnation and curses to that city. That is why God made that law. We cannot rehabilitate sin. Criminals do not need to be protected. We need to deal with the root problem in our nation, which is denial of the things of God. The only thing to do is to stop making excuses for murder and rape. That's the only solution. It does not matter if we are in the grace administration. We still have curses coming down on us because we let people go. They get paroled and repeat the same crime again and again.

Let's quit trying to think that people who are dealing drugs and things like that are all right. Let's get

SELF IMPOSED CURSES

honest with what they are. They are the breath of Satan, and if they don't repent, they are wasting our air. If we, as a nation, would take a stand against evil, guess what would happen to evil? It would at least thin down a bit, right?

In our nation it really does not make a difference, even murderers go free. They go free because of a technicality. They did not get asked the right thing, or they are the right color, so they got by with it. Now there is talk about having quotas for the electric chair. There cannot be any more people put to death than the percentage of races in our country. What does that have to do with sin? It's a sad thing. Sin is the enemy of all of us. It's the enemy against our God. These are things we need to repent of for the sake of our nation.

(Deuteronomy 19:13) Thine eye shall not pity him, but thou shalt put away the guilt of innocent blood from Israel, that it may go well with thee.

Israel's final destruction in 70 A.D. happened because they cheered to see the innocent blood of Jesus spilled. They said, "Crucify him, crucify him!" Free the wicked and kill the innocent! Yet the same thing is going on in our country today.

There is a cry going up to heaven, to God. It is the blood of forty million babies that have been killed. Other than the innocence we have through the new birth, there is not anything more innocent than the blood of a baby that's still in its little waterbed, called the womb. The baby should not be violated in the womb. We need to repent. Let's quit making excuses, because this is an important issue to face up to and to repent.

These are very serious curses and the punishment for not repenting is death, probably sooner than later. Maybe you don't think that nowadays these things apply, but I can only tell you that I have seen hundreds of people set free from disease, from poverty, from mental illness, from too many other evil things. Once the curses are broken off, the change is dramatic; it's almost immediate!

Don't think for one minute that because the Old Testament has so much to say about curses and blessings that we don't have to be concerned about them now. Some people say, "Oh, the Old Testament is past and even the New Testament has gone by. We're in the 21st century—there are no more curses. Lighten up!" Talk about being deceived! These people sure are.

We should not take lightly what God tells us in the Old Testament. There is a saying that goes: "The Old Testament is in the New revealed, and the New Testament is in the Old concealed!" The entire Bible is talking about the same subject: salvation that comes from the one true God. He always was, He is, and He always will be the same. God made a way for us to be free from the curses that are on us. That way is the salvation that came through the Lord Jesus Christ, the

SELF IMPOSED CURSES

only-begotten Son of God, the Messiah, and it covers people all the way from Adam to our children, our grandchildren, and our children's descendants. For our sakes, Jesus Christ took upon Himself the curse of sin, which was death.

(Isaiah 53:5-6) But he was wounded for our transgressions, he was bruised for our iniquities: the chastisement of our peace was upon him; and with his stripes we are healed.
All we like sheep have gone astray; we have turned every one to his own way; and the LORD hath laid on him the iniquity of us all.

When people turn to the Lord and get rid of their curses and blessings are put in their place, it is a powerful thing. The tears of joy and repentance are tremendous. Hollywood could never reproduce something like this. These curses can go on for many generations. For instance, the curse on Israel is still there; they are still being persecuted. But those who have repented and removed the curse are not being persecuted. It's fun to be around Messianic Jews. They can really praise the Lord. They have found their Messiah and repented from the errors of their fathers.

Self-imposed curses go on and on until we make the decision to stop them. We need to repent and to ask God to help us and to give us blessings instead of

TURNING CURSES TO BLESSINGS

curses. The need for repentance will go on until the end of the world as we know it, and Satan is totally destroyed. The Bible says, in Revelation 22:3 that in that day: **There shall be no more curse: but the throne of God and of the Lamb shall be in it; and His servants shall serve him.** Praise God for the option of repentance!

Chapter 11
The Curse of Poverty

What is the curse of poverty? What causes the curse of poverty? In Haggai chapter 1, God's people were guilty of having nice homes and letting the temple fall apart. In this day and time, the temple is the Body of Christ and we are still guilty of not taking care of that temple.

(Haggai 1:6) Ye have sown much, and bring in little; ye eat, but ye have not enough; ye drink, but ye are not filled with drink; ye clothe you, but there is none warm; and he that earneth wages earneth wages to put it into a bag with holes.

Here in America, we have little sayings like, "I owe, I owe, it's off to work I go," or, "Too much week left at the end of my paycheck." Our poverty is always somebody else's fault. But that is not what God's Word says. Shall we believe how we feel, or believe what God says?

It is interesting how the Lord introduces the context of the tithe. He knew that we would be stingy, so He reminds us that He is the Lord and He does not change.

TURNING CURSES TO BLESSINGS

(Malachi 3:6) For I am the LORD, I change not; therefore ye sons of Jacob are not consumed.

We are the sons of Jacob. If Abraham is our father of faith and we want to have his blessings, then we obviously are the sons of Jacob.

(Malachi 3:7) Even from the days of your fathers ye are gone away from mine ordinances, and have not kept them. Return unto me, and I will return unto you, saith the LORD of hosts. But ye said, Wherein shall we return?

We should not go away from God's ordinances. But if we have, we must return unto Him. Then we don't have to run all over trying to find God and His blessings. He will return to us.

(Malachi 3:8) Will a man rob God? Yet ye have robbed me. But ye say, Wherein have we robbed thee? In tithes and offerings.

Tithe simply means a tenth. To give an offering would be to go beyond ten percent. The prophet Jeremiah said, "Cursed is the man that trusts in man," yet the first fruit of our check is withheld in taxes. Many people think that they are tithing, when they give a tenth of what they bring home. If we are to be

THE CURSE OF POVERTY

free from the curse of poverty, we need to give at least a tenth of all our increase.

(Malachi 3:9) Ye are cursed with a curse: for ye have robbed me, even this whole nation.

Do you think that the curse being talked about here is from Satan? If Satan could bless you, he would do it for withholding from God. Let's face it, this curse is from God. We self-impose this curse by hanging on to what belongs to God.

(Malachi 3:10) Bring ye all the tithes into the storehouse, that there may be meat in mine house, and prove me now herewith, saith the LORD of hosts, if I will not open you the windows of heaven, and pour you out a blessing, that there shall not be room enough to receive it.

God gives us both our portion and His together so that we can either prove Him and see His abundance. Or we can withhold His ten percent and live in poverty. We get to choose. The curse of poverty is like a double-edged sword. It is a form of idolatry when we love money more than we love the Lord. We don't show appreciation to Him by giving. It is a form of idolatry and idolatry brings curses. And that's why poverty and idolatry go hand in hand. In the nations where you see the greatest poverty, there are many idols and few Christians.

(Malachi 3:11) And I will rebuke the devourer for your sakes, and he shall not destroy the fruits of your ground; neither shall your vine cast her fruit before the time in the field, saith the LORD of hosts.
And all nations shall call you blessed: for ye shall be a delightsome land, saith the LORD of hosts.

In America, we have droughts, floods, crop failures, and disasters. At one time, the whole world knew that we were a Christian nation and they feared us. We are not seeing the blessings in this day that we had in times past. We do not have the abundance of food, or the respect of the world. In verse 7, it says, "If you return unto me, I will return unto you." Wake up, church! We need to repent and to see our nation rise back up again because of God's blessings. No wonder we don't strive to get our children to continue in the church. We don't even invest back to God what is His. So, if we will not trust Him with our money, we will not trust Him with our children. This could cause them an eternity in hell.

Chapter 12
Jesus Was Made a Curse For Us

At first I didn't pay any attention to the little six-year-old boy, I was just too busy praying for people. But he kept jumping around and waving his arms and shouting aloud. I was in Bucharest, Romania in February 1998, and had just finished speaking to a big group of people in one of the churches there. As I usually do afterwards, I was praying for people. The little boy kept coming around, jumping and waving his arms, shouting "Alleluia" and "Slava Domnului" (meaning, "Praise the Lord"- in Romanian). I would smile at him and then try to ignore him, but he kept jumping around and waving his arms and shouting aloud.

Finally, someone told me that this little six-year-old was one I had prayed for during a visit the year before. He was mute. At that time, I had asked the Lord to remove the curses on him and put great blessings where there used to be that curse. When I realized who the little boy was, then I was the one shouting, "Hallelujah, praise the Lord!" You can't see any more clearly that a curse has been removed than with children who have been delivered from them. Children are generally so spontaneous and expressive that you can see the difference right away.

Another time I was with the gypsies, and a little girl probably nine or ten years old, kept hanging onto

TURNING CURSES TO BLESSINGS

my arm, pulling at my shirt, holding my hand and staying with me. She was trying to tell me something. I couldn't figure out what she was saying because she was talking in gypsy. I found out later that she was a little girl from whom I had removed curses. God had healed her cleft palate (a hole in the roof of her mouth) and her lip, which was terribly deformed. That was what she was trying to tell me. She just wanted to share her healing with me and to say thank-you.

About a year later when I returned to the church she attends, I saw her again. There she was—this little girl who had been healed of her cleft palate and her deformed lip—now singing beautifully. She is one of the main members of the music team at her church. The amazing thing about her singing was that before, even her speech could not be understood because the sounds came up through her nose.

The way curses operate in people's lives is very real. What great sin did the six-year-old boy do that he should have been cursed with a spirit of dumbness? Do you think the little girl with the hole in the roof of her mouth got that way because she did something bad? No, she was born that way. Even doctors recognize that condition as generational, or inherited. But in God's mercy, He has given the way out. Just because something is inherited, does not mean it has to be that way for the rest of your life.

There is a good Christian couple in Romania who had been trying for eighteen years to have children. Everyone had prayed for the couple without success.

JESUS WAS MADE A CURSE FOR US

In 1997, they asked me to pray for them. I talked to the Lord and asked Him how to pray for them. Then the Lord showed me to remove a curse that was in their lives. Almost a year later, the couple came to me while I was visiting on another missionary trip. They came to ask me to dedicate their new baby to the Lord. They had the child they had wanted so desperately. Talk about the mercy of God! It makes me cry to think how loving our God is.

I have hammered the issues about curses very hard because it makes us recognize that curses really exist. The problems caused by curses are far more widespread than we have realized. But we don't just want to identify a problem. We want to find the solution. Complete deliverance is available to you and to me, because of what our Lord Jesus Christ did for us. That's why the following verse is one of my favorites.

(Galatians 3:13) Christ hath redeemed us from the curse of the law, being made a curse for us: for it is written, Cursed is every one that hangeth on a tree:

The Romans didn't pick up the prettiest pole, all varnished and clean, to hang Jesus on. That tree had maggots on it from rotting blood, vile blood of vile men who had died on it before. Jesus had to die in the most cursed way. In Christianity, we know that Jesus' blood washes away our sin. We know that He died

TURNING CURSES TO BLESSINGS

and rose again. We also know He ascended and we understand the power of His name. But we lost track of the reason why He died the way He died.

Have you ever wondered why He hung on a tree, rather than dying in some other way? He died on a cross to remove those curses—those strongholds and those ways in which the devil can legally get into your life. That's why Jesus died that way. If it had been necessary to have a Mack truck run over him, either it would have been invented in that day or He would have waited a while to come and do what He did.

The abuse He went through the night before—every thing the Romans did to Him was awful. They did everything they could to kill him beforehand. He was locked up with a group of soldiers that were so vile that they even enjoyed murdering babies with their mothers watching in horror. Jesus had to fight to hold onto His life. He had to die on the cross so that you and I could have our curses removed.

It would have been so much easier for Jesus to die before he was hung on the cross. He hung on and did not let go of His life until He was on the cross. And then He gave his life. He GAVE his life—they couldn't kill Him! That is how determined Jesus has been for you, and He still is determined for you. If He went that far for you, why would you think that He could not deliver you today, or your children, or your nation? Cursed is everyone who hangs on a tree. The other men who were hung on the tree deserved it.

JESUS WAS MADE A CURSE FOR US

To be crucified was absolutely the worst, most cursed way to die. No mother would have been proud to see her son die that way. The crowds jeered, they made fun and they spit on Him. The shame and reproach that he bore is almost incomprehensible. It's a tragedy in Christianity that, because of our pet doctrines, we say that Christians can't be cursed. We still hold to that doctrine even after all He went through. Jesus was blameless and yet died in the worst way possible. Why did He allow it?

(Galatians 3:13-14) Christ hath redeemed us from the curse of the law, being made a curse for us: for it is written, Cursed is every one that hangeth on a tree:
That the blessing of Abraham might come on the Gentiles through Jesus Christ; that we might receive the promise of the Spirit through faith.

(Isaiah 53:5-6) But he was wounded for our transgressions, he was bruised for our iniquities: the chastisement of our peace was upon him; and with his stripes we are healed.
All we like sheep have gone astray; we have turned every one to his own way; and the LORD hath laid on him the iniquity of us all.

TURNING CURSES TO BLESSINGS

All of our iniquities were laid on Jesus and He paid the price for our sin. He didn't make one excuse—we make excuses. That is one of our iniquities. Jesus went the whole route. We must believe that if there is something He wants us to do, we will be able to do it and we can do it—no excuses.

When Joshua was told by God, "Moses, my servant, is dead," God told him to get up and get going and go take the land. Jesus was hung on the tree to be cursed for us. But if we don't get up and fight for our freedom from curses, we're still going to have them. By His stripes, we were healed. Then why are we sick? Because we have to fight for our health. We have an enemy and his purpose is three-fold: to steal, to kill, and to destroy. Which one of these do you like? I don't like any of them! I choose none, thank you.

Back in Washington State in 1989, I got some kind of poisoning in my system. I was praying, but I kept getting sicker. Pretty soon, I started turning yellow and I knew that my liver was giving me a lot of trouble. We were still praying. My friends were telling me, "Carl, this is not like a kidney problem. You have two kidneys, but you only have one liver. If it fails, you die. You need to go see a doctor." I kept saying, "I am healed by Jesus' stripes, and I don't need any doctor!" And God bless Sheila, my wife. She stood with me on this. I was so weak that I couldn't get out of bed and for six days, I was in and out of a coma.

JESUS WAS MADE A CURSE FOR US

One day when I was all alone, I heard a laugh and a voice saying, "Why don't you let loose? You're going to die!" It was Satan. I said, "I am going to let it loose. I am going to give it to God. I have been trying to make my faith happen. Either God heals me, or I will die. I don't care. It is His problem." But I kept getting weaker.

Then, suddenly I saw my wife's face right in front of mine and felt her tears dripping on my face. She said, "I'm sorry, honey, I called 911." This stirred me up and I found enough strength to get out to my pickup truck. I headed off the mountain that we lived on and I drove up to the high Cascade logging country. I wanted to get to one of my favorite spots there, where I'd had good times talking things over with God.

I had to walk the last hundred yards to get a view of Lake Spada. I would go a few feet and then fall in exhaustion. I heard that same laughter again and a voice said, "Now you're going to die, because nobody knows where you are." And I said, "I don't care. Something has to change! I either get healed today in the name of Jesus, or the coyotes will have me for supper!" I fell asleep on the ground. When I woke up, my strength had returned. My skin was still yellow, but I was praising God! I jumped in my pickup and roared down those logging roads to get home.

When I reached Highway 2, I noticed a family whose car had broken down. I was so blessed; I wanted to help them. I said, "Let me get your car started." They looked at me. I hadn't shaved or bathed for six days and I was yellow. I could understand their fear. I said, "I'm healed, I'm healed. Jesus healed me! But if you don't believe me, get upwind from me." And they did.

I'm not sure what I did to their car, but it started. And I said, "God bless you, I need to get home." I left them standing upwind. A mile down the road, before I made the last turn behind the mountain, they were still standing upwind by the car. I'm sure they are not there now!

When I got home, we had great rejoicing. Sheila told me that she had called 911 but had not let me know because she knew how I felt about it. She had gone to lead the ambulance to our place because they didn't know how to find us in the mountains. She was not even home at the time that I thought I saw her face next to mine. Praise the Lord! It must have been God who gave me the vision of her face, so I would get moving.

Sometimes we have a hard time believing that everything is taken care of. I believe that when we are sick, the doctor should not be our first call. Our first call should be to God in the name of Jesus Christ. Then we can go get the aspirin bottle or whatever is needed. **"But seek ye first the kingdom of God and his righteousness (Matthew 6:33)."** By Jesus' stripes, we were healed. If we can believe this, we can truly be blessed. Even if the doctor helps us, God is still the healer.

JESUS WAS MADE A CURSE FOR US

It's an amazing thing, because when you remove curses, God will also give you the revelation of the blessing that is needed. And then, that blessing starts ministering in place of the curse. You know, sometimes a year will pass after someone was prayed for and had curses removed and blessings put in their place. Then they'll call me and I have to go back and try to remember who it was and what we did. Then they tell me what they were into before and how God has changed their lives. Sometimes you cannot even recognize the person. I'm talking about people who were bi-polar manic-depressives, insane, all kinds of things.

The first time we dealt with insanity was in a church with a man who was bi-polar. The man did not get healed right away, but there was evidence of change. Then he called me up and told me he was going to quit taking lithium. Bi-polar people are supposed to take this medicine for life.

So, I said, "Well, why don't you just start cutting back on it?"

The man said, "Carl, you don't understand. You don't cut back on lithium. If you go off of it, you have a chance that you will go completely insane. You either take it or you don't. And if I've making a mistake, I'm going to go in faith, but I won't know it until it happens. I feel led of the Lord."

So, I said, "I sure can't advise you, Brother, but whatever you decide to do, I will stand with you."

TURNING CURSES TO BLESSINGS

He said, "I called you because I knew you would stand with me. I've already decided and I have been off of the lithium for four days already. Anytime in six weeks I may go overboard."

For those six weeks, I was praying for the man. When Satan could no longer affect his mind, he attacked the man's kidneys. They collapsed. His whole renal system shut down. We prayed in the name of Jesus Christ and he received new kidneys and God honored our prayer.

This man has gone through so many trials. He is one of the strengths in that church today. He is a strong counselor there. I had no idea when we dealt with this kind of insanity, how things would go. The blessings keep working, even though the devil is committed to try to steal them away. But those blessings are ministering at every beat of the heart. Those blessings will stay there unless we kick them out.

There is only one way to get rid of curses. That is death. Do you want to get rid of your curses? Die! The Bible instructs us to die to ourselves, right? Jesus died on the cross and He took the curses. But we have to die to ourselves; we have to die to our flesh in order to stay free from curses. I am talking to myself on this issue also. What we really need to remember is that God does care. He has a burning love for us, even though sometimes we don't have this kind of love for Him.

JESUS WAS MADE A CURSE FOR US

Christ has redeemed us from the curse of the law, being made a curse for us: "Cursed is every one that hangeth on a tree:" **If we will walk in Christ, we will be curse-proof!**

(Galatians 3:14) That the blessing of Abraham might come on the Gentiles through Jesus Christ; that we might receive the promise of the Spirit through faith.

Faith is very important here. If we believe that His promise is greater than our problem, we will receive the promise of God. It takes faith to trust that God has a solution. As we have said so many different ways throughout this book, we need to repent, to ask forgiveness for our sins and the sins of our forefathers, so that even the generational curses can be broken.

(1 John 1:8-10) If we say that we have no sin, we deceive ourselves, and the truth is not in us.
If we confess our sins, He is faithful and just to forgive us our sins, and to cleanse us from all unrighteousness.
If we say that we have not sinned, we make Him a liar, and His word is not in us.

Write your name on this one! Is there anyone reading this who does not sin? This verse is here because we do sin. When we sin, we leave ourselves open for the enemy to cause us to be cursed. But we have an advocate with the Father who is standing ready to represent us before the throne of God.

(1 John 2:1) My little children, these things write I unto you, that ye sin not. And if any man sin, we have an advocate with the Father, Jesus Christ the righteous:

We're going to stumble if we don't love one another. That's why the devil tries so hard to get us to judge one another. After all, if I can find a sin in you, you don't dare confront me because I can slap you back. This goes on among God's people! Who do you think orchestrated that one?

(Romans 12:9-10) Let love be without dissimulation. Abhor that which is evil; cleave to that which is good.
Be kindly affectioned one to another with brotherly love; in honour preferring one another;

One day I was driving down the road and had a vision. I saw a big tube coming down, obviously from Heaven, and there were good things coming out of it—blessings. As I looked, the blessings started going right back up the tube just that quickly! Reversed—going away! And then I saw some little hooks that were hooking them. So, I said, "God, what is this?" He said, "Those hooks are unforgiveness. I love my people. I bless my people. I answer their prayers. But there are things they are doing which gives Satan the legal right to steal those things away. It does not really matter if they say 'I'm sorry'."

Do you want to get rid of curses in your life? Start forgiving! We are supposed to forgive. There will always be someone doing something bad to us, but it is our responsibility to forgive and it is to our benefit. You can't say that you love someone if you can't forgive him or her. We all have to work on loving one another. This is what makes it tough, but we have to get involved with one another. Are you having difficulty getting along with someone? Spend some time with them. Do them a favor. If we would work on getting along with one another, it would make a big difference.

This whole book on "Turning Curses to Blessings" can be summarized in one word: **LOVE**.

(1 Corinthians 13:13) And now abideth faith, hope and charity, these three; but the greatest of these is charity.

The greatest thing we can do is love. That will open the door to freedom. If we really love people, we are not going to be afraid to tell them about Jesus. If we really love people, we are not going to be afraid

TURNING CURSES TO BLESSINGS

to offer them healing. We need to take this kind of stand. "The greatest of these is love."

Chapter 13
A New Beginning

It is time we stopped claiming all kinds of reasons why we have curses on us. There are only two reasons: 1) not listening to God, and 2) not obeying His Word.

(Deuteronomy 28:1, 2) And it shall come to pass, if thou shalt hearken diligently unto the voice of the LORD thy God, to observe and to do all his commandments which I command thee this day, that the LORD thy God will set thee on high above all nations of the earth:
And all these blessings shall come on thee, and overtake thee, if thou shalt hearken unto the voice of the LORD thy God.

If your effort is to obey and to hearken diligently to the voice of God's Word, blessings will seek you out and they will not be lost. They overtake you!

HOW DO I KNOW IF I'VE BEEN CURSED?

We need to look out for curses in our own lives and in those of others. We have to bring the work of Satan out into the open. That's why Jesus came to this

TURNING CURSES TO BLESSINGS

earth. He came so that He could destroy the works of the devil.

(1 John 3:8) For this purpose the Son of God was manifested, that he might destroy the works of the devil.

The following list is helpful to use as a checklist of symptoms that can indicate the presence of curses. Take this list and check through your own life and your family. If these symptoms are prominent in your life, you need to repent of any sin in your life and in your ancestors, and break the curses.

Humiliation
Physical illness
Family breakdown
Poverty
Mental illness
Destruction
Defeat
Oppression
Depression
Failure
Fear of Failure
Disfavor from God
Mental exhaustion
One sickness after another
Divorce
Miscarriages
Female problems

A NEW BEGINNING

Female problems
PMS
Infertility
Family always fighting
Poverty
Things always going wrong
Accidents looking for a place to happen
Deceived
Being deceived

THE CURE

THE SOURCE OF THE CURE IS GOD.

THE ONLY WAY TO THE CURE IS JESUS.

DEATH ON THE CROSS WAS AND IS THE ONLY PRICE THAT WAS PAID FOR THE CURE.

HOW TO REMOVE CURSES

In Deuteronomy 28:1-2 we have the promise that if we shall hearken diligently to the voice of the Lord, we shall have the blessings overtake us. However, in Deuteronomy 28:14, it says, **"if thou wilt not hearken unto the voice of the LORD thy God, to observe to do all his commandments and his statues which I command thee this day; that all these**

TURNING CURSES TO BLESSINGS

curses shall come upon thee, and overtake thee."

I exhort you with all my strength and heart to read from verse 15 until the end of Deuteronomy 28. If you see any of these curses in your life or in your family, pray to God in Jesus' name and repent for any unforgiven sins that you or your generations before you have done to cause these curses. Command the curses to be broken in the name of Jesus Christ and speak blessings to replace the curses in the name of Jesus. We have written out the entire passage in Appendix 1, so that you can logically and constructively deal with these matters that have had destructive consequences in your life.

This is not a religious experience. It is a spiritual preparation for you to serve your God, to be good parents, to be good spouses, and to be a great witness to a world that is dying in its curses. As these blessings start to minister to you, day-by-day, you will see changes. You will feel stronger, your confidence in your relationship with the Lord will be stronger, and your family ties will be sweeter. Financial blessings generally take some time, but as you are faithful to do what the word of God calls you to do, you will also see blessings in this area.

My prayer for each person that is reading this book is for his or her life to change, to move closer to the center of God's will, to be that witness that we are asked to be in God's Word. Our confidence in God

A NEW BEGINNING

will continue to grow until we can say to that mountain, "Be thou removed," in the name of Jesus and see it come to pass.

Please allow me to pray with you: Heavenly Father, in the name of our Lord Jesus Christ, we come before you with praise and thanksgiving for the marvelous work that you have done for us. You gave your only-begotten Son, our Savior, to die on Calvary's cross and to suffer such torture, so that we could be your children. You paid the price that it cost for all of our sins and the disobedience that we continue to do in our lives. Thank you right now for breaking the power of that sin in our lives and setting us free from any curses that have held us in bondage. We ask this in the name of Jesus for ourselves and for our families. We repent for the sins of our ancestors and of our nation. We ask that you will cleanse us with the blood of Jesus Christ as white as snow. Thank you that you will remember those sins no more. We humbly ask that you will help us to continue to obey your word, to seek your face, and to love and love some more. Thank you for all of the wonderful blessings of rest, health, prospering in your way, being able to bless those who curse us, being able to forgive and be forgiven. Thank you for encouraging us to speak your promises against any problem that we have. Give us faith that is greater than our problems. Help us to forgive those we have not forgiven, even if they have cursed us. We repent

TURNING CURSES TO BLESSINGS

for any occult or occultist practices in our lives and in our families, or anything that we have permitted to get into our lives that have led us away from making your Son, Jesus, our Lord. Give us the strength to glorify your name in all situations, to give the sacrifice of praise and thanksgiving in place of complaint and discouragement. We thank you, Heavenly Father, for all that you have done in our lives and are going to do, in the name of our Lord Jesus Christ. Amen.

Appendix 1
Deuteronomy 28:15-68

28:15 But it shall come to pass, if thou wilt not hearken unto the voice of the LORD thy God, to observe to do all his commandments and his statutes which I command thee this day; that all these curses shall come upon thee, and overtake thee:
28:16 Cursed shalt thou be in the city, and cursed shalt thou be in the field.
28:17 Cursed shall be thy basket and thy store.
28:18 Cursed shall be the fruit of thy body, and the fruit of thy land, the increase of thy kine, and the flocks of thy sheep.
28:19 Cursed shalt thou be when thou comest in, and cursed shalt thou be when thou goest out.
28:20 The LORD shall send upon thee cursing, vexation, and rebuke, in all that thou settest thine hand unto for to do, until thou be destroyed, and until thou perish quickly; because of the wickedness of thy doings, whereby thou hast forsaken me.
28:21 The LORD shall make the pestilence cleave unto thee, until he have consumed thee from off the land, whither thou goest to possess it.
28:22 The LORD shall smite thee with a consumption, and with a fever, and with an inflammation, and with an extreme burning, and with the sword, and with blasting, and with mildew: and they shall pursue thee until thou perish.
28:23 And thy heaven that is over thy head shall be brass, and the earth that is under thee shall be iron.
28:24 The LORD shall make the rain of thy land powder and dust: from heaven shall it come down upon thee, until thou be destroyed.
28:25 The LORD shall cause thee to be smitten before thine enemies: thou shalt go out one way against them, and

TURNING CURSES TO BLESSINGS

	flee seven ways before them: and shalt be removed into all the kingdoms of the earth.
28:26	And thy carcase shall be meat unto all fowls of the air, and unto the beasts of the earth, and no man shall fray them away.
28:27	The LORD will smite thee with the botch of Egypt, and with the emerods, and with the scab, and with the itch, whereof thou canst not be healed.
28:28	The LORD shall smite thee with madness, and boldness, and astonishment of heart:
28:29	And thou shalt grope at noonday, as the blind gropeth in darkness, and thou shalt not prosper in thy ways: and thou shalt be only oppressed and spoiled evermore, and no man shall save thee.
28:30	Thou shalt betroth a wife, and another man shall lie with her: thou shalt build an house, and thou shalt not dwell therein: thou shalt plant a vineyard, and shalt not gather the grapes thereof.
28:31	Thine ox shall be slain before thine eyes, and thou shalt not eat thereof: thine ass shall be violently taken away from before thy face, and shall not be restored to thee: thy sheep shall be given unto thine enemies, and thou shalt have none to rescue them.
28:32	Thy sons and thy daughters shall be given unto another people, and thine eyes shall look, and fail with longing for them all the day long: and there shall be no might in thine hand.
28:33	The fruit of thy land, and all thy labours, shall a nation which thou knowest not eat up; and thou shalt be only oppressed and crushed always:
28:34	So that thou shalt be mad for the sight of thine eyes which thou shalt see.
28:35	The LORD shall smite thee in the knees, and in the legs, with a sore botch that cannot be healed, from the sole of thy foot unto the top of thy head.

APPENDIX 1

28:36 The LORD shall bring thee, and thy king which thou shalt set over thee, unto a nation which neither thou nor thy fathers have known; and there shalt thou serve other gods, wood and stone.

28:37 And thou shalt become an astonishment, a proverb, and a byword, among all nations whither the LORD shall lead thee.

28:38 Thou shalt carry much seed out into the field, and shalt gather but little in; for the locust shall consume it.

28:39 Thou shalt plant vineyards, and dress them, but shalt neither drink of the wine, nor gather the grapes; for the worms shall eat them.

28:40 Thou shalt have olive trees throughout all thy coasts, but thou shalt not anoint thyself with the oil; for thine olive shall cast his fruit.

28:41 Thou shalt beget sons and daughters, but thou shalt not enjoy them; for they shall go into captivity.

28:42 All thy trees and fruit of thy land shall the locust consume.

28:43 The stranger that is within thee shall get up above thee very high; and thou shalt come down very low.

28:44 He shall lend to thee, and thou shalt not lend to him: he shall be the head, and thou shalt be the tail.

28:45 Moreover all these curses shall come upon thee, and shall pursue thee, and overtake thee, till thou be destroyed; because thou hearkenedst not unto the voice of the LORD thy God, to keep his commandments and his statutes which he commanded thee:

28:46 And they shall be upon thee for a sign and for a wonder, and upon thy seed for ever.

28:47 Because thou servedst not the LORD thy God with joyfulness, and with gladness of heart, for the abundance of all things;

28:48 Therefore shalt thou serve thine enemies which the LORD shall send against thee, in hunger, and in thirst,

TURNING CURSES TO BLESSINGS

and in nakedness, and in want of all things: and he shall put a yoke of iron upon thy neck, until he have destroyed thee.

28:49 The LORD shall bring a nation against thee from far, from the end of the earth, as swift as the eagle flieth; a nation whose tongue thou shalt not understand;

28:50 A nation of fierce countenance, which shall not regard the person of the old, nor show favour to the young:

28:51 And he shall eat the fruit of thy cattle, and the fruit of thy land, until thou be destroyed: which also shall not leave thee either corn, wine, or oil, or the increase of thy kine, or flocks of thy sheep, until he have destroyed thee.

28:52 And he shall besiege thee in all thy gates, until thy high and fenced walls come down, wherein thou trustedst, throughout all thy land: and he shall besiege thee in all thy gates throughout all thy land, which the LORD thy God hath given thee.

28:53 And thou shalt eat the fruit of thine own body, the flesh of thy sons and of thy daughters, which the LORD thy God hath given thee, in the siege, and in the straitness, wherewith thine enemies shall distress thee:

28:54 So that the man that is tender among you, and very delicate, his eye shall be evil toward his brother, and toward the wife of his bosom, and toward the remnant of his children which he shall leave:

28:55 So that he will not give to any of them of the flesh of his children whom he shall eat: because he hath nothing left him in the siege, and in the straitness, wherewith thine enemies shall distress thee in all thy gates.

28:56 The tender and delicate woman among you, which would not adventure to set the sole of her foot upon the ground for delicateness and tenderness, her eye

APPENDIX 1

shall be evil toward the husband of her bosom, and toward her son, and toward her daughter,

28:57 And toward her young one that cometh out from between her feet, and toward her children which she shall bear: for she shall eat them for want of all things secretly in the siege and straitness, wherewith thine enemy shall distress thee in thy gates.

28:58 If thou wilt not observe to do all the words of this law that are written in this book, that thou mayest fear this glorious and fearful name, THE LORD THY GOD;

28:59 Then the LORD will make thy plagues wonderful, and the plagues of thy seed, even great plagues, and of long continuance, and sore sicknesses, and of long continuance.

28:60 Moreover he will bring upon thee all the diseases of Egypt, which thou wast afraid of; and they shall cleave unto thee.

28:61 Also every sickness, and every plague, which is not written in the book of this law, them will the LORD bring upon thee, until thou be destroyed.

28:62 And ye shall be left few in number, whereas ye were as the stars of heaven for multitude; because thou wouldest not obey the voice of the LORD thy God.

28:63 And it shall come to pass, that as the LORD rejoiced over you to do you good, and to multiply you; so the LORD will rejoice over you to destroy you, and to bring you to nought; and ye shall be plucked from off the land whither thou goest to possess it.

28:64 And the LORD shall scatter thee among all people, from the one end of the earth even unto the other; and there thou shalt serve other gods, which neither thou nor thy fathers have known, even wood and stone.

28:65 And among these nations shalt thou find no ease, neither shall the sole of thy foot have rest: but the

TURNING CURSES TO BLESSINGS

           LORD shall give thee there a trembling heart, and failing of eyes, and sorrow of mind:

28:66   And thy life shall hang in doubt before thee; and thou shalt fear day and night, and shalt have none assurance of thy life:

28:67   In the morning thou shalt say, Would God it were even! and at even thou shalt say, Would God it were morning! for the fear of thine heart wherewith thou shalt fear, and for the sight of thine eyes which thou shalt see.

28:68   And the LORD shall bring thee into Egypt again with ships, by the way whereof I spake unto thee, Thou shalt see it no more again: and there ye shall be sold unto your enemies for bondmen and bondwomen, and no man shall buy you.

About the Author

Carl Fox, serving the Body of Christ for over 25 years, has ministered to thousands throughout the United States from Washington and Oregon to Maine and Massachusetts, as well as India, Romania, and the Ukraine. He has also started and pastored churches in Minnesota, New Mexico, California, and Washington. By teaching, preaching, and praying for healing, he has been able to build people up and learn how to stop the enemy's attacks, receiving freedom to rise up and serve the Lord. By His grace, God has empowered Carl to impart a greater understanding and ability in areas of the ministry of the Spirit.

He purposes to prepare the church for the last days, that we may be a blessing to the Lord. His life and ministry can best be explained by his faith in the Word of God and his determination to walk in the Spirit without the limitation of structured religious systems that try to dictate what may or may not be done.

By equipping the saints to stop the enemy's attacks, ministries are freed to help each other in the bond of peace and unity. As the importance of each individual to the Body of Christ is brought to light, many are enabled to rise up and serve the Lord.

Carl lives in Truth or Consequences, New Mexico, with his wife Sheila, and oversees the work of Christian Faith International Ministries.

Order Form

Tape Sets and CD's on Turning Curses to Blessings and many other materials and books are available to order from Christian Faith International. Please see our bookstore on the website: www.cfim.net

Turning Curses to Blessings
3-tape set $22.00
CDROM $30.00

Name_____
Address_____
City, State, Zip_____
Telephone #_____

Amount Enclosed_____

Shipping & Handling included in price.

Send to:
Christian Faith International
412 Grape St.
Truth or Consequences NM 87901
505-894-5691
Email: carlcfi@zianet.com